D1356925

Prayers for This Life

Prayers for This Life

Edited by

CHRISTOPHER HOWSE

continuum
LONDON • NEW YORK

Continuum
The Tower Building, 11 York Road, London SE1 7NX
15 East 26th Street, New York NY 10010

www.continuumbooks.com

© Christopher Howse 2005

First published 2005

British Library Cataloguing-in-Publication Data
A catalogue record for this book is available from the British Library.

ISBN 0-8264-7642-2

Typeset by Kenneth Burnley, Wirral, Cheshire
Printed and bound in the UK by Cromwell Press, Wiltshire

Contents

Introduction   xi

PART ONE: GOD

1. God himself
A Hebrew word: Alleluia   2
Id ipsum   *Augustine of Hippo*   2

2. Creation worships God
Brother Sun   *Francis of Assisi*   8
God loves creation   *Julian of Norwich*   9
Mermaid and quince adore   *Christopher Smart*   10
In the playful fire   *Ananias, Azarias and Misael*   12
God loves me   *Frederick William Faber*   14
God made me lovable   *Thomas Traherne*   15
We seek your face   *Alcuin*   18
We praise God to know him   *Augustine of Hippo*   19
My body and soul's praise   *Anselm*   20
Worthy the winning   *Gerard Manley Hopkins*   20
Creator, grant the prize   *John Henry Newman*   21

3. Speaking with God
Preparation for prayer   *Lancelot Andrewes*   23
Met half way   *James Montgomery*   25
Give ear to our prayers   *Book of Common Prayer (1549)*   26
Want more   *Thomas Traherne*   26
Grant our desires   *John Chrysostom*   27
The First Commandment   *Thomas Ken*   28
Quietness   *Book of Common Prayer*   34
Finding God within   *Walter Hilton*   34
Praying for things   *Book of Common Prayer*   35
Inner healing   *John Keble*   36
A brisk example   *Christopher Smart*   36
God's will in me   *George MacDonald*   39

4. Our Father

The Lord's Prayer   40
Seven askings   *William Caxton*   40
In heaven and my heart   *Girolamo Savonarola*   42
On earth as in heaven   *Thomas Traherne*   43
Debitoribus nostris   *John Kettlewell*   45

PART TWO: GOD WITH US

5. God becomes man

Come, Emmanuel   *J. M. Neale*   48
Wake up   *John Henry Newman*   49
Word made flesh   *The Angelus*   50
Midnight sun   *Giles Fletcher*   51
What the shepherds saw   *John Byrom*   52
The Nativitie of Christ   *Robert Southwell*   52
Wonderful exchange   *The Missal*   53
Sharing in Divinity   *Columba Marmion*   54
Triple epiphany   *Liturgy of the Hours*   55
Giving to God   *Christina Rossetti*   55
Life of Jesus   *Book of Common Prayer*   56
To take God's side   *Frederick William Faber*   57

6. Cross and resurrection

The paschal mysteries   *Book of Common Prayer*   58
Agony in the Garden   *Ronald Knox*   58
The world's life   *Alcuin*   59
Our sins nailed   *Orthodox Liturgy of the Hours*   60
The most peculiar thing   *Thomas Traherne*   60
Tree of life   *Venantius Fortunatus*   62
Second Adam   *John Henry Newman*   64
The Passion Chorale   *Henry Baker*   65
Empathy   *Anselm*   66
Sword of sorrow   *Jacopone da Todi*   67
Dying with Christ   *Book of Common Prayer*   68
Love so amazing   *Isaac Watts*   68
Hide me in thy wounds   *Anima Christi*   69
The sign of the cross   70
Before a crucifix   71

Christ is risen   *The Missal*   71
Easter   *Book of Common Prayer*   72
Easter dialogue   *Joseph Beaumont*   72

7. Eucharist
Let us give thanks   *The Missal*   75
Love's welcome   *George Herbert*   76
Bread of angels   *Liturgy of the Hours*   77
The present Trinity   *The Missal*   77
Act of confidence   *Lady Lucy Herbert*   78
Be heartened   *John Keble*   78
Jesus' presence   *Thomas Aquinas*   79
Friend and brother   *Richard of Chichester*   81
Unity   *Richard Challoner*   81
Jesus Christ the Apple Tree   *Christina Rossetti*   82
Countless gifts   *Catherine Winkworth*   83

8. Reconciliation
With a great cry   *Anon, AD 1000*   84
Intolerable burden   *Book of Common Prayer*   85
Rend my rocky heart   *Thomas Traherne*   86
Act of contrition   *Traditional*   87
New hearts   *Book of Common Prayer*   87
Three fatal sisters   *Robert Herrick*   88
Becoming whole   *George MacDonald*   88
Deliver us   *Book of Common Prayer*   89
Jesus lost   *Richard Challoner*   89
In peril on the sea   *Book of Common Prayer*   93
None should perish   *Christina Rossetti*   93
God's promises   *Book of Common Prayer*   94
No outcast   *John Keble*   94
Bodily suffering   *Book of Common Prayer*   94
Coolness and balm   *J. G. Whittier*   95
As we forgive those . . .   *Book of Common Prayer*   96
For enemies   *Anselm*   96
In my bosom a sun   *Henry Vaughan*   97

9. The Holy Spirit
The Comforter   *Book of Common Prayer*   98
Dwell in me   *Anselm*   99

Light of life   *John Austin*   100
Sent by the Trinity   *William Caxton*   101
Steadfast repose   *George Hickes*   103

10. Communion of saints

In God's eye, Christ   *Gerard Manley Hopkins*   104
One body   *John Donne*   105
Gifts in each member   *John Keble*   109
A nesting place   *Christina Rossetti*   110
Lighting us   *Henry Vaughan*   111
All generations   *Book of Common Prayer*   112
Sub tuum praesidium   *Traditional*   113
Fertile tears   *Aldhelm*   113
An angel's message   *Book of Common Prayer*   114
Our Lord and Our Lady   *Hilaire Belloc*   114
Star of the sea   *Alcuin*   115
Salve   *Hermann Contractus*   116
All seafarers   *John Paul II*   116
Remember   *Traditional*   117

11. Angels

Heaven and earth   *Book of Common Prayer*   118
They walk with us   *Augustine Baker*   118
Guardian angel   *Anonymous*   120
My oldest friend   *John Henry Newman*   120
Fellow-servants   *Christopher Smart*   122
St Michael   *Leo XIII*   123

PART THREE: THIS LIFE WITH GOD

12. The presence of God

God be in my head   *Anonymous*   126
Dwelling in hearts   *Anonymous*   126
In me and outside   *Augustine of Hippo*   127
Christ's hand   *R. H. Benson*   128
A new colour   *Ronald Knox*   129
Living like a candle   *John Bunyan*   130
Divine friendship   *Thomas Traherne*   132
Knowing Jesus   *John Henry Newman*   132

13. Faith, hope and love

The Apostles' Creed *Traditional*	138
An act of hope *John Gother*	139
Comfort and hope *Book of Common Prayer*	140
St Francis's plank *Lady Lucy Herbert*	141
God is where love is *The Missal*	141
For charity *Book of Common Prayer*	142
Wants and love *Thomas Traherne*	142
Neutrality loathsome *Robert Herrick*	144
Kindness *Jane Austen*	144
Our pattern *Jeremy Taylor*	145
Lovest thou me? *William Cowper*	146
God in the poor *Christina Rossetti*	147
Fruit *Mother Teresa*	148

14. Daily life

Important hours *Jane Austen*	149
Save us, now *Book of Common Prayer*	149
One step enough *John Henry Newman*	150
Against perils *Book of Common Prayer*	151
God's power *Anonymous*	151
The Captain *Christina Rossetti*	154
After a quarrel *The Seafarers' Prayer Book*	154
An instrument *Anonymous*	155
Martha, Martha *Robert Herrick*	156
Grace before meals *Traditional*	156
A visit *William Walsham How*	157
In loneliness *The Seafarers' Prayer Book*	159
No more lies *Susanna Wesley*	160
For self-forgetfulness *Robert Louis Stevenson*	161

15. Morning and night

This day *Lancelot Andrewes*	162
The morning-watch *Henry Vaughan*	167
Dawn *Liturgy of the Hours*	168
Night prayer *Alcuin*	169
Lighten our darkness *Book of Common Prayer*	169
Family prayers *John Wesley*	169
A continuance of mercies *Jane Austen*	171
In wakefulness *The Seafarers' Prayer Book*	172

Shadows sink   *Hannah More*   173
Unfathomable mines   *William Cowper*   173
The evening   *Lancelot Andrewes*   174

16. This life completed
Sure and certain hope   *Book of Common Prayer*   180
Let me see Thy face   *Augustine of Hippo*   181
Repair me now   *John Donne*   181
Vain terrors   *Samuel Johnson*   182
In the hour of death   *Book of Common Prayer*   183
No cold love   *Thomas More*   183
The condemned man   *John Gother*   185
Last affliction   *William Dodd*   186
Judgement   *Liturgy of the Hours*   187
The Book of Life   *Christina Rossetti*   189
Heaven and hell   *Thomas Traherne*   190
Lead me home   *John Newton*   191
Resurrection of the body   *St Patrick*   191

Sources and further reading   193

Introduction

This book is meant for people who want to pray: but for reasons to be given, there is no intention of telling you the best way for you to pray. You will find here short prayers, prayerful poetry and some meditative passages on connected themes, taken from authors of the past 2,000 years.

The outlook is from an English-speaking viewpoint, and the prayers chosen are those that have entered the English-speaking Christian tradition. There are great riches in other places – the Eastern churches, the Jewish tradition and Islam most obviously – and people do pray faithfully whose idea of God is very different from the Christian one. But I think a package tour of unfamiliar cultures can make for a shallow kind of spiritual globetrotting. You can't just pick the pretty prayer flags outside the Tibetan monastery and leave untried the hard discipline of the monks inside.

Instead of a voyage round the world I have travelled through time, for the centuries bring insights that strike us anew because of their unfamiliarity, yet seem to remind us of something we had once been told. The impressive literary merits of much prayerful prose and poetry from the past arrest the attention, and the slight strangeness of vocabulary provides ideas in unhackneyed terms. In any case, there is an infinite exploration to be undertaken within the Western tradition; literally so, for it claims to be in touch with the infinite on a personal level: there are people at either end of the conversation. As George Herbert puts it with his jagged paradox, prayer is an

> Engine against the Almighty, sinner's tower,
> Reversed thunder, Christ-side-piercing spear.

So, then, if the prayers in this volume are there to be used, this is not a manual in the sense of a 'How to' book. Only one rule applies to everyone: pray every day. Beyond this, to demand a specific method of everyone is an impossibility, and it is an impertinence to specify the way in which someone should pray. It is worse than telling them how they should eat, for with prayer not only does the choice of diet depend on the individual make-up, but the underlying process of digestion and nourishment is not of our doing at all. If prayer is the lifting up of the heart and mind to God, the mechanics of the lifting process are beyond us, and the things that happen to the heart and mind once lifted are the work of the Holy Spirit.

This might sound abstract or alarming, but as it happens, the supernatural is the most natural thing in the world. Though God is a burning furnace of pure act, he is kind and tender in his actions towards us. The Holy Spirit is less often apparent as tongues of fire or a mighty rushing wind than as a suave, gentle, gradual, quiet, inward and friendly presence, sometimes unnoticed. When we think we can't pray, he prays in us.

Hence, although contemplation and mental prayer may sound élitist and difficult, many busy mothers, working men, careless teenagers or lonely old people – the usual stereotypes – have been praying in close union with God without knowing it. Even though they suppose their prayers are merely vocal, these people grow into temples of the Holy Spirit when, with good intentions in their hearts, they make themselves available to him. Christians are familiar with the insight of St Paul: 'We know not what we should pray for as we ought, but the Spirit itself maketh intercession for us with groanings which cannot be uttered.' Everyone has this personal tutor, of whose actions they need not be explicitly aware.

That is why vocal prayers, prayers made out of words, spoken or perhaps written, are not despicable. They can be part of that extra-ordinary elevation of our deepest selves to take part in the internal life of God.

I am not talking about prayers recited as if they were the shipping forecast, with no intention of their being directed to God. And verbal prayers may lack that direction for more reasons than lack of intention. The wicked Claudius in *Hamlet* kneels on stage (while Hamlet is wondering whether to stab him then and there) and after a while gets up, saying, 'My words fly up, my thoughts remain below./Words without thoughts never to heaven go.' It is not just that Claudius said 'Our father' and found that the words meant nothing, never touched his mind, and were lost in distraction. That can happen to anyone. His trouble (and we can impute motives to him freely since he is a fictional character) was that he didn't really want to pray. He didn't even want to ask God to sow repentance in his heart. He was still intent on his morally bad plotting 'below'.

Yet despite finding it hard sometimes to pay attention to prayers that are known by heart, these can 'work', in four ways.

First, they can be said straightforwardly, aloud or to ourselves, and mean just what they say. One can say the Lord's Prayer, the 'Our Father', like that, although, if one is at the same time monitoring whether one is paying attention, it is a hundred to one against getting to the end with much awareness of what each petition means.

To say the Lord's Prayer involves bringing to it the results of our having pondered it in our hearts, meditated upon it in periods set aside for quiet prayer and, most likely, having read some useful commentary on it or heard a speaker bringing out meanings that would not have occurred to us.

But there is a practical virtue in sometimes saying this prayer and others straight through at a set pace, alone or with other people, for to do so keeps the mind trotting with a purpose instead of wandering from the path, looking for rabbits in the long grass.

Secondly, familiar prayers can be made to 'work' by using them as prompts during a period of mental prayer. All I mean by 'mental prayer' is the few minutes that a lot of people like to set aside each day when they can be alone with God, considering his presence and conversing, as it were, mentally. But on some occasions, nothing comes to mind; or at least, what comes to mind has nothing much to do with God. So a piece of meditative writing that we have to hand can be resorted to, and before long we find ourselves praying again, and the book can be shut or set to one side for a while. Sometimes an author whose book we are reading outside the time set aside for prayer expresses an idea at some length. That is how John Donne works in the long passage about the bell tolling that I have included; but once that idea is in our minds, even a short reference to that long passage will bring to remembrance what it was all about. Similarly a little phrase from a well-known prayer can pull thoughts back to God. Classic writers on prayer often liken such short prayers to the kindling that gets a fire going.

Since this period of prayer alone with God requires us to be open to his promptings, there is no point filling it up with pre-made prayers. That is like stacking the hallway from floor to ceiling with chairs; when the knock comes on the door it is impossible to open it. But equally there is no point sitting in an empty hall waiting, while listening to loud music to pass the time. That way, we won't hear the knock. A few words from familiar prayers, which we know are about the expected guest, calm our fidgets and remind us what it is that we can converse with him about.

The same goes for gaps at church. If we go to church services there are gaps between sections of 'action', gaps when no words are being said, and the people involved are walking from one place to another or interminably adjusting microphones. Since we are used to television, such breaks in action are usually an opportunity to make a cup of coffee or feed the cat. Otherwise we get that uncomfortable sensation of waiting around, as in a supermarket queue. But in church it is quite different. The little gaps of inaction are where we come in. Since the mind is elastic, and unfinished business (the shopping list, that name we couldn't remember earlier) bounces into our consciousness the moment the lid is lifted on its jack-in-the-box, it is as well to have ready a painless prompt to keep it from rapidly becoming absent entirely. If there is a service book or leaflet, the prayers there should help. If not, then there are prayers in the memory, either from church services (some of which are very beautiful) or from our habitual stock (some of which have associations particular to us alone).

Thirdly: by a paradox, formulas of prayer can be used by not paying attention to their words. That might sound shocking. But, in the Eastern Christian tradition, the 'Jesus prayer' is used in this way. The person praying settles down quietly to saying, calmly and repeatedly, 'Lord Jesus Christ, Son of God, have mercy on me, a sinner.' Of course, the person praying does mean the words, but while the outer mind is occupied in reciting them, the 'deeper' mind or soul is left free to regard God, to believe in him, love him and be open to him.

This might sound too mystical, but, in a slightly different way, since this other practice intentionally employs the imagination, it is only what pious people do when they recite the rosary. There the vocal prayers are recited while a series of scenes is considered from the life of Jesus Christ – the announcing of his birth, his presence in his mother's womb when she visits her cousin Elizabeth, his birth, his presentation in the Temple, and so on.

This technique not only keeps the recitative parts of the body and brain innocently occupied, but also fills the imagination with pictures of the greatest relevance to Christian prayer, for Christianity is a doubly incarnational religion. It is founded on the fact of God becoming man, or rather it is founded by a person who is God and man; and secondly it is a religion for human beings to whom God brings good things while they are walking about as flesh and blood. In the rosary, as in other exercises of imaginative meditation, both Jesus the Son of God and ourselves as thinking human beings are implicitly present. In the rosary, the person praying stands beside Jesus's mother Mary, a human being who has empatheticaly accompanied her son through his life on earth.

The fourth way of using familiar prayers is to allow them to express our own spontaneous responses to God during the day or night. Novelists have attempted to represent the 'interior monologue' of human consciousness, though it seldom makes interesting reading. But if a human being is in the presence of God, there is an interior dialogue. We are not talking to ourselves but to God, and of course we must be careful not to talk as if to God but still be talking to ourselves, just as we must not treat God as an 'imaginary friend' that does not exist, or talk to him as if he were the cat, a mere sounding board that does not understand and have feelings for us.

Yet there is no need to be anxious about whether we are really addressing God or not in our thoughts, for he is present all the time in reality, and comes to our aid. He does not let the batteries of our mobile phones run down, and there is no tunnel that breaks up our audibility. Walter Hilton, in the fourteenth century, knew the value of keeping in contact with God during the day, as he explained in his book, *The Ladder of Perfection*:

> There is another sort of vocal prayer which is not by any set common form of prayer; but is, when a man or woman, by the gift of God, feeling the grace of devotion, speaks to God, as it were, bodily in His presence, with such words as suit most his inward stirrings at the time, or as come to his mind, matching the feelings or motions of his heart. It might be by expressing his sins and wretchedness, or the malice and tricks of his enemy, or of the mercies and goodness of God. And so he cries out with the desire of his heart and the speech of his mouth to our Lord for aid and for help, as a man who is in peril among his enemies. Or in sickness, showing his maladies to God as to a doctor, saying with David: 'Deliver me from my enemies, O Lord.' Or: 'Heal my soul, for I have sinned against Thee'; or other suchlike words as they come to his mind.

Sometimes a verse of the Psalms expresses exactly what one wants to say – as thanks, or petition, or praise, or contrition. Or it could be just something we have often said to God: 'Teach me to love.' That might not come from Scripture but be our own invention, or at least seem our own invention. Other such exclamations come from something we have read or heard, which we make specially our own because it speaks to us. We remember it because it means something at a particular time in our lives. It doesn't have to be expressed as a petition. It can be a statement: 'God is good.' Such statements have their meanings, and the meaning is not abstract when there is someone apart from the speaker who hears it.

I mentioned the Psalms as a source of phrases that can come to mind as spontaneous prayers during the day. That is because in most Christian traditions the Psalms are central to repeated acts of worship. The Psalms bridge the divide between East and West, Protestant and Catholic. They are recited unaccompanied by instrumental music in Benedictine monasteries and Calvinist meetings. Many people know whole series of Psalms by heart. But I have not included them here, otherwise I should have to include them all. You will find phrases from the Bible in this book, and most of the prayers here are related to the Bible. But I have made the self-denying ordinance of excluding detached quotations from the Bible, apart from a canticle or two, such as the Magnificat, that stand as anchor-points for the liturgy.

Go to Evensong at St Paul's Cathedral in London or to Vespers at Notre Dame in Paris and you will hear the Magnificat sung. 'It is an excellent and fruitful custom of holy Church that we should sing Mary's hymn at the time of evening prayer', wrote Bede 1,300 years ago. 'By meditating upon the incarnation, our devotion is kindled, and by remembering the example of God's Mother, we are encouraged to lead a life of virtue. In the evening we are weary after the day's work and worn out by our distractions. The time for rest is near, and our minds are ready for contemplation.'

Poetry does not, however, have to be scriptural to express things in a seemingly more heartfelt way than our own invented phrases. Somehow, just because it comes from outside, a poem – by George Herbert, say, or Gerard Manley Hopkins – seems to put our own feelings more strongly than we can contrive. We recognize in the poet's lines ideas we had only half formed. 'Yes, that is what I feel too', we exclaim, and we remember the words.

Hymns are even more memorable than verse, thanks to the prompting of the tune. They also benefit from an unexpected privilege: their quality as poetry does not have to be so very high in order for them to serve as stimuli of prayer. A phrase from 'Amazing Grace' or 'Dear Lord and Father of mankind' can pierce the resistance of familiarity, and the same is true of many a less felicitous hymn. 'The people called Methodists were supposed by their Founder to have many uses for good hymns besides singing them in public assemblies', says the preface from an augmented collection of Wesley's hymns published in the 1870s. 'Here also will be found some adapted to personal and private, rather than to collective worship, or to praising the Lord secretly among the faithful, rather than in the congregation.' Wesley's hymns are used in other churches too, just as Methodists have drawn into their hymn books compositions by ancient writers from a quite different habit of worship.

I have not hesitated to include a few hymns and verses in Latin. Now that people can listen with pleasure to a reconstruction of Monteverdi's Vespers of 1610, sitting comfortably with a cup of coffee at home, there seems no reason to pretend that a few lyric passages from old devotional Latin hymns are impenetrably difficult. A phrase such as *Peto quod petivit latro poenitens* – 'I make the same request as the penitent thief' (the good thief on the cross), from the eucharistic hymn attributed to Thomas Aquinas, is as memorable as the first words of the old Mass, *Introibo ad altare Dei* – 'I shall go unto the altar of God.'

At the other end of the historical spectrum from ancient prayers are what I would call 'teatowel prayers'. One (not included here) called 'Desiderata', beginning 'Go placidly', is reproduced not only on teatowels but also on cards, bookmarks and laminated wall posters. It often bears the note 'Found in St Paul's church, Baltimore, 1692'. But the language is not that of the seventeenth century, which is hardly surprising, since it was composed in 1927 by one Max Ehrmann from Indiana. In 1956 it was circulated by the incumbent of St Paul's Baltimore, a church which indeed traces its foundation to 1692. Another example is the so-called 'Seventeenth-century Nun's Prayer' ('I am growing older and will some day be old'), and another was supposed to have been found in the locker of an old woman in hospital. These teatowel prayers, or meditations, are folksy and appealing, and they are propagated on their own merits.

It is surprising perhaps that many modern prayers are hard to pin on a definite author. The so-called 'Serenity Prayer', associated with Alcoholics Anonymous, but used very widely by people who are unaware of the connection, seems to have been written by Reinhold Niebuhr, but even he was not absolutely certain that it did not derive from an older source.

A discovery for me during the compilation of this anthology was about the 'Prayer of St Francis', with its series of opposition 'Where there is . . .' lines. When Margaret Thatcher recited part of it outside 10 Downing Street one day when she was Prime Minister, some people were shocked that she should take to herself the words of the unworldly St Francis. They need not have worried on that narrow count, for the prayer was composed only in 1912 – the most successful teatowel pretender of all, though written in all innocence. It is so good, I have included it in this book.

You will not find here much in the way of prayers addressed to saints. Some people object to them on principle. I cannot quite see the logic of this when they ask the saints to intercede on our behalf to ask for good things from God. It seems to me that if you can ask someone alive on earth to pray to God for you, there is nothing wrong with asking a saint in heaven to pray for you. God wishes to be asked for things, or he would not have asked us to pray for them, as he does, often, in the Bible. So in the chapter on the Communion of Saints, I have included some prayers addressed to the Virgin Mary. One of them, the 'Sub tuum praesidium', dates from the third century or before. During his life on earth, Jesus was persuaded to perform his first miracle, to turn water into wine at the marriage feast at Cana, at his mother's request. 'This beginning of miracles did Jesus in Cana of Galilee,' St John remarks, 'and manifested forth his glory; and his disciples believed in him.' Just so, any involvement of the Mother of Jesus in the life of prayer manifests the glory of God, the source of all gifts, and the same goes for the proper use of devotion to other saints. But which personal devotions you have is a matter of choice. Perhaps it might sound something like superstition to someone, but I have never met anyone who hasn't found that St Anthony of Padua is useful in finding things that are lost: the car keys in the fridge, the stolen car in a street, a passport brought to the airport and so on.

The strict standards of the Book of Common Prayer are far more accommodating to the idea of the helping hands of angels. Angels are in fashion these years, though I shudder at some New Age ideas about them. The Bible is quite definite about their activity as servants of God. The most ancient eucharist prayers envisage a cosmic liturgy, in which the redeeming action of God is surrounded by angels worshipping. How often these immensely powerful and intelligent spiritual creatures are made in some way visible to our eyes is not certain. It is reasonable to think that we do not always recognize them.

An angel is mentioned at the conclusion of Jesus's prayer in the garden of Gethsemane. Elsewhere we are told of Jesus going into a deserted place to pray, but in Gethsemane just before his death, we actually hear something of how he himself prayed, in earnest and extremity. That is why a picture, or icon, of Jesus praying there appears on the front cover. He is a person who prays as a human, like us. His prayer is for this life, for this very day on which he lives, a human. He asks, if it is possible, not to have to go through the terrible experience of the cross, but he adds the proviso, 'Not my will but thine be done.' In that sentence he makes his own will as a human accord with the will that he possesses as God. It is not that God wills a bad end for Jesus. God's will is free, but his choice is not between good and evil but between different courses of good.

We call 'providence' the good choices that God makes to bring good results from ill circumstances. Providence and God's own self are one and the same thing. In conforming his own decisions to those of God, Jesus holds fast to the rescue that God plucks from the wickedness attempted at the Crucifixion, the murder of God. The rescue is not just for Jesus, who as man rises from the dead, but for all those with whom he is showing solidarity in choosing to undergo the death they have earned – in other words, for every man and woman.

After his death, Jesus, as depicted by ancient Christian artists, particularly in the East, plucks Adam and Eve by the wrists and pulls them from the graves they had dug for themselves. With that firm grasp they are uprooted from the dead earth and grafted as branches onto him, the vine. He is the new stock, the new Adam, from which all humanity will draw life. This is all the consequence of Jesus's prayer in Gethsemane. It was no light thing for Jesus to ask that the will of God be done, but it was the only way in which humankind could be remade in Christ. It also made it possible for us, as bidden, to pray the words 'Thy will be done' and to know that God's beneficent will for us is not thwarted. Our prayer brings us within the rescue plan for this our earthly life.

God remains with us in this life and draws prayer out from us like a magnet. Nothing whatsoever can prevent prayer. A mother constantly caring for children can pray. Someone going through painful surgery can pray. If you are stuck in a bus with a video playing, you can pray. There are bound to be distractions, even in a quiet cloister. This life is the one in which we learn to pray.

Christianity is a demanding religion. We are commanded to do something impossible for us: to love God with our whole hearts. 'The act of prayer clarifies and purges our heart', St Augustine writes, 'and makes it more capable of receiving the divine gifts that are poured out for us in the spirit.' We possess an unquenchable thirst for the love of God. And yet when we let our buckets down on a string to fetch out the water that can quench our thirst, all we get is a cupful at a time, it seems, if we are lucky. The Samaritan woman at Jacob's well had just the same problem, and she heard the answer: 'Everyone who drinks of this water will be thirsty again, but those who drink of the water that I will give them will never be thirsty. The water that I will give will become in them a spring of water gushing up to eternal life.'

The Samaritan woman asked for that water, and in prayer we are like the Samaritan woman, engaging Jesus in conversation, not quite understanding what he tells us. We do not have much to bring to a conversation with God, but when we can't think what to say, to know some prayers by heart helps, as does reading prayers that the best and holiest minds have contrived. Those are what I have looked for, and I hope others will find them useful.

Christopher Howse
London, 2005

PART ONE

God

1
God himself

A Hebrew word: Alleluia

Alleluia: Praise ye the Lord.

The Hebrew word occurs in the Psalms, and is picked up in the last book of the New Testament, Revelation or the Apocalypse. It has been used ever since in Christian worship. The element at the end of the word represents Ja, 'God', Yahweh, 'He who is', the description of God given to Moses at the burning bush, as told in Exodus 3:14.

Id ipsum
Augustine of Hippo

In peace in the selfsame I will sleep, and I will rest
In pace in id ipsum dormiam et requiescam. (Psalm 4)

A striking example of how two words from the Bible can live in someone's heart, with a significance that others miss, is to be found in the vigorous writings of Augustine of Hippo (354–430). The two words (sometimes written as one) are 'id ipsum', *which come in Psalm 4.*

I think the meaning of these two words for Augustine is worth examining in unusual detail because it illustrates so well how a holy and intelligent man used things he had read to feed his life of prayer.

In his short autobiographical book, Confessions, *Augustine relived the experience of reading the fourth psalm at a critical time in his life, when, aged 32, he had given up his successful career and was staying in the country while contemplating his next step. He began to read this psalm, and experienced a great insight when he came to the words* id ipsum – *the self-same – which are applied in the psalm to God, in whom the psalmist discovers the rest that Augustine was seeking. Augustine found, when reading this verse for the first time, that it entered his heart, and he began to shout it aloud.*

Towards the end of the Confessions *he returns to the words, which provoke in him another outburst of adoration of God: Holy, Holy, Holy.*

After this initial discovery, for the rest of Augustine's life, the words id ipsum *in the Scriptures conveyed to him God's unchanging nature. This he saw as 'Being-Itself', the I AM WHO AM which God gives as his name in Exodus 3:14. In his commentary on Psalm 121, Augustine was to dwell on the sentence,* Hierusalem quae aedificatur ut civitas cuius participatio eius in id ipsum *(Jerusalem, which is built as a city, which is compact together), again taking* 'id ipsum' *as God, in whom Jerusalem finds stability.*

While Augustine never ceases to wonder at God as 'Being in Itself', he finds the thought incomprehensible and, as a Christian, he returns after a while in his thoughts about this psalm to the Incarnation, the Word made Flesh. God as id ipsum *'is too much to understand', Augustine writes. 'Hold on instead to what he whom you cannot understand became for you. Hold on to the flesh of Christ, on to which you, sick and helpless, left wounded and half dead by robbers [a reference to the parable of the Good Samaritan] are hoisted, that you may be taken to the inn and healed there.'*

For most modern Bible-readers, the words id ipsum *will not have jumped out at all, because Augustine was using a different translation of the psalm in question. The version he used derived from the Greek Septuagint – the translation made for Jews living in the diaspora before the birth of Christ. Jerome, Augustine's contemporary, made a new translation from the original Hebrew, but it was the Latin version based on the Greek Septuagint that remained the 'Vulgate' edition in common use, until it was revised afresh for liturgical use in 1948. The Hebrew version of the Psalms, though, was to be the one on which in 1611 the Authorized Version in English most relied. So Psalm 4 in the Authorized Version does not correspond to the text which made such an impression on Augustine.*

Here, then, is Psalm 4 in the Douay translation from the Vulgate published in 1609, and below it Augustine's account of how he was struck by the psalm.

Psalm 4

1 Unto the end, in verses. A psalm of David.
2 When I called upon him, the God of my justice heard me: when I was in distress, thou hast enlarged me. Have mercy on me: and hear my prayer.
3 O ye sons of men, how long will you be dull of heart? Why do you love vanity, and seek after lying?

4 Know ye also that the Lord hath made his holy one wonderful: the Lord will hear me when I shall cry unto him.

5 Be angry, and sin not: the things you say in your hearts, be sorry for them upon your beds.

6 Offer up the sacrifice of justice, and trust in the Lord: many say, Who sheweth us good things?

7 The light of thy countenance O Lord, is signed upon us: thou hast given gladness in my heart.

8 By the fruit of their corn, their wine and oil, they are multiplied.

9 In peace in the selfsame I will sleep, and I will rest:

10 for thou, O Lord, singularly hast settled me in hope.

Confessions Book 9, Chapter 4

Now the day had come when I was indeed free from my professor-ship of Rhetoric, from which in my mind I was free already. And it was done. You, Lord, rescued my tongue from the same thing from which you had already rescued my heart. And I blessed you, rejoic-ing, and went away, with all those close to me, to the house in the country.

My books show what I did there by way of writing. I was now wholly at your service, though still as it were, breathless after a round in the school of pride. Some of my writing was debated with my friends there, some with myself alone, before you. What I wrote to the absent Nebridius, my Letters bear witness.

And when shall I have time to detail all the great things you did for us at that time? For I hurry on to yet greater mercies. And I find it very pleasant to be prompted by my memory to confess to you, O Lord, the spurs by which you inwardly tamed me, and how you ironed me out, bringing down the mountains and hills of my thoughts, straightening my crookedness, and smoothing my rough ways. And how you also reconciled the brother of my heart, Alypius, to the name of your only begotten Son, our Lord and Saviour Jesus Christ, which he would not at first allow to be inserted in the things we wrote. For he preferred them to smell of the cedars of the Schools, which the Lord has now broken down, than of the whole-some herbs of the Church – the antidote against serpents.

How I cried out to you, my God, when I read the Psalms of David, those songs of faith, those sounds of devotion, which allow no pride of spirit. I was still unlearned in true love for you, a catechumen resting in that house in the country, with Alypius, a catechumen too, my mother inseparably sticking to us. Womanly in appearance, she had the faith of a strong man, the tranquillity of age, the love of a mother, the piety of a Christian.

How I cried out to you in those psalms. And how they kindled my feelings for you. I burnt to recite them, if I could, through the whole world, against the pride of mankind. And so they are sung, through the whole world, and no one can hide from your fire.

How strongly, with what bitter sorrow, I grew angry at the Manichees. Yet I pitied them, for they knew nothing of those sacraments, those medicines, but raged madly against the antidote which might have cured them of their madness. I wish they could have been somewhere there nearby me, without my knowing, to have seen my face and heard my words, when, in that time away, I read the fourth Psalm.

How that Psalm affected me: 'When I called upon you, you heard me, the God of my justice. You have enlarged me in my distress. Have mercy on me, O Lord, and hear my prayer.' I wish they could have heard what I said on reading those words, but without my knowing they heard, lest they should think I spoke for their sakes. (For in truth I should not have said the same things, in the same way, if I had perceived that they heard and saw me. Nor when I spoke them would they have taken them in the same way as when I spoke by and for myself before you, out of the natural feelings of my soul.)

I shivered with fear, then boiled again with hope and rejoiced in your mercy, Father; and my eyes and my voice gave expression to these feelings. All the while your good Spirit turned to us, and said, 'O ye sons of men, how long will you be dull of heart? Why do you love vanity, and seek after lying?' For I had loved vanity, and sought after lying. And you, O Lord, had already made 'your holy one wonderful', raising him from the dead and setting him at your right hand, whence from on high he should send his promise, the Comforter, the Spirit of truth. And he had already sent him, but I knew it not; he had sent him, because he was now made wonderful, rising again from the dead, and ascending into heaven. For till then, the Spirit was not yet given, because Jesus was not yet glorified.

And the prophet cries out, 'How long will you be dull of heart? Why do you love vanity, and seek after lying? Know ye also that the Lord hath made his holy one wonderful.' He cries out, 'How long?'

5

He cries out, 'Know this.' And I so long, not knowing, loved vanity, and sought after lying. And therefore I heard and trembled, because it was spoken to such as I remembered myself to have been.

For in those phantoms which I had held for truths, there was vanity and lying. And I roared out many things, earnestly and forcibly, in the bitterness of my remembrance. I wish they had heard me, those who yet love vanity and seek after lying! They would perhaps have been troubled, and have vomited up their poison; and so you might have heard them when they cried to you. For by a true death in the flesh did he die for us, the one who now makes intercession to you for us.

I read on: 'Be angry, and sin not.' How moved I was, O my God, having now learned to be angry at myself for things past, so I might not sin in future. Yes, justly angry; for it was not an alien nature of people of darkness which sinned through me, as the Manichees say (who are not angry at themselves, and treasure up wrath against the day of wrath and of the revelation of your just judgement).

Nor was my good any longer outside me, to be sought with the eyes of flesh under the earthly sun. For those who seek joy from outside soon become foolish, and waste themselves on visible and temporal things, and in their famished thoughts they do lick their very shadows. Oh, I wish they were wearied out with their famine, and said, 'Who showeth us good things?' And they would hear us say, 'The light of thy countenance O Lord, is signed upon us.' For we are not that light which enlightens every man [John 1:9], but we are enlightened by you. Having been darkness, we may be light in you. Oh, that they could see the internal Eternal Light – which having tasted, I was sorely troubled that I could not make them see, even though they brought me their heart in their eyes (always roving abroad from you) and said, 'Who showeth us good things?'

There I was, angry within myself in my own room, inwardly pricked. I had offered my sacrifice, slaying my old self and beginning purposefully on a new life, putting my trust in you. You had begun to grow sweet to me there, and had 'given gladness in my heart'. And I cried out, as outwardly I read this, finding it struck home inwardly. Nor did I want worldly goods 'multiplied' – wasting away time, and being wasted by those temporal things. Instead I had in your eternal simple essence other 'corn, wine, and oil'.

And with a loud cry from my heart I shouted aloud the next verse: 'Oh, in peace in the selfsame I will sleep, and I will rest.' Oh, what did the psalmist say – I will lie down and sleep, for who shall stop us, when it has come to pass the sentence that is written, 'Death is swallowed up in victory'?

And you above all are the Self-same, you who are not changed. And in you is rest which forgets all toil, for there is no one else apart from you. Nor are we to seek the many other things which are not what you are. But 'thou, O Lord, singularly hast settled me in hope'.

Confessions, Book 12

'Out of nothing God made heaven and earth.'

But where did it gain this degree of being from, but from you, Lord? From you all things are, insofar as they have being. The less like you they are, the further they are from you – though it is not the distance of place. For you, Lord, are not one thing in one place, and another thing in another place. No, you are the Self-same, and the Self-same, and the Self-same. Holy! Holy! Holy! Lord God Almighty, in the beginning, which came from you, in your wisdom, which was born of your own substance, you created something, and that out of nothing. For you created heaven and earth – not out of yourself, for then they would have been equal to your only begotten Son, and thus equal to you too. No, it is not right that anything is equal to you which did not come from you. Nothing else was there but you O God – one Trinity, and triune Unity – for you to make anything from. So out of nothing you created heaven and earth – a great thing, and a small thing – for you are Almighty and Good, to make all things good, the great heaven, and the little earth.

2

Creation worships God

Brother Sun
Francis of Assisi

Most High, all powerful, good Lord,
Yours is the praise, the glory, the honour, and all blessing.
To you alone, Most High, do they belong, and no man is
    worthy to speak your name.

Be praised, my Lord, through all your creatures,
especially through my lord Brother Sun.
He brings the day, and you give light through him.
He is beautiful and radiant in great splendour.
Of you, Most High, he bears the likeness.

Praised be you, my Lord, through Sister Moon and the stars.
In the heavens you formed them, bright and precious and
    beautiful.

Praised be you, my Lord, through Brother Wind,
and through the air, stormy or fair,
and every kind of weather through which
    you give sustenance to your creatures.

Praised be you, my Lord, through Sister Water,
So useful and humble and precious and pure.

Praised be you, my Lord, through Brother Fire,
through whom you light the night.
He is beautiful and playful and robust and strong.

Praised be you, my Lord, through Sister Earth.
She sustains us with her fruits and flowers of many colours and
    herbs.

Praised be you, my Lord, through those who pardon for the
 sake of your love,
and bear infirmity and trials.
Blessed are those who endure in peace,
 for they shall be crowned by you, Most High.

Praised be you, my Lord, through our Sister Bodily Death,
from whom no living man can escape.
Woe to those who die in their sins!
Blessed are those that she finds doing your will.
No second death can do them harm.

Praise and bless my Lord,
and give him thanks
and serve him with great humility. Amen.

*Francis of Assisi (1181–1226) began to compose this canticle after he had
received the stigmata, the marks of Jesus's crucifixion, on his body, and was
suffering greatly. 'I want', he said, 'to compose in his praise a new hymn
about the Lord's creatures, of which we make use each day, without which we
cannot live, and with which the human race greatly offends its Creator.' The
concluding verses, about Sister Death, were sung by his brothers as Francis
was dying.*

God loves creation
Julian of Norwich

Our Lord showed me a spiritual vision of his familiar loving.
 I saw that he is to us everything that is good and comfortable.
 He is our clothing that for love wraps us, clasps us, and for tender
love encloses all about, so that he may never leave us. He is to us
everything that is good, as I understand it.
 Also at this time he showed me a little thing the size of a hazelnut
in the palm of my hand; and it was as round as a ball.
 I looked at it with the eye of my understanding, and thought:
What may this be?
 And it was answered thus: It is all that is made.
 I marvelled that it should last, for I thought it might suddenly
have fallen into nothing, it was so small.

And I was answered in my understanding: It lasts, and ever shall last because God loves it.

And so everything has its being by the love of God.

In this little thing I saw three properties.

The first is that God made it,

The second is that God loves it,

The third, that God keeps it.

This forms part of one of the sixteen 'showings' from Jesus seen interiorly by Julian (born 1342), and recorded in her short book Revelations of Divine Love. *She had made her home as an anchoress or hermit in a cell next to the church of St Julian in Norwich, from which she takes her name, and her level-headed advice was sought by contemporaries seeking closer friendship with God.*

Mermaid and quince adore
Christopher Smart

For ADORATION all the ranks
Of angels yield eternal thanks,
    And DAVID in the midst;
With God's good poor, which last and least
In man's esteem, thou to thy feast,
    O blessed bridegroom, bidst.

For ADORATION seasons change,
And order, truth, and beauty range,
    Adjust, attract, and fill:
The grass the polyanthus checks;
And polish'd porphyry reflects,
    By the descending rill.

Rich almonds colour to the prime
For ADORATION; tendrils climb,
    And fruit-trees pledge their gems;
And Ivis with her gorgeous vest,
Builds for her eggs her cunning nest,
    And bell-flowers bow their stems.

With vinous syrup cedars spout;
From rocks pure honey gushing out,
    For ADORATION springs;
All scenes of painting crowd the map
Of nature; to the mermaid's pap
    The scaled infant clings.

The spotted ounce and playsome cubs
Run rustling 'mongst the flow'ring shrubs,
    And lizards feed the moss;
For ADORATION beasts embark,
While waves upholding halcyon's ark
    No longer roar and toss.

While Israel sits beneath his fig,
With coral root and amber sprig
    The wean'd advent'rer sports;
Where to the palm the jasmine cleaves,
For ADORATION 'mongst the leaves
    The gale his peace reports.

Increasing days their reign exalt,
Nor in the pink and mottled vault
    The opposing spirits tilt;
And, by the coasting reader spi'd,
The silverlings and crusions glide
    For ADORATION gilt.

For ADORATION rip'ning canes
And cocoa's purest milk detains
    The western pilgrim's staff;
Where rain in clasping boughs enclos'd,
And vines with oranges dispos'd,
    Embow'r the social laugh.

Now labour his reward receives,
For ADORATION counts his sheaves
    To peace, her bounteous prince;
The nect'rine his strong tint imbibes,
And apples of ten thousand tribes,
    And quick peculiar quince.

These stanzas on adoration come from the great poem by Christopher Smart (1722–71) called 'A Song to David', which was composed during the years 1757 to 1763, when he was kept at St Luke's Asylum. Though he was confined on the grounds of madness, even during his period in asylums he wrote poetry of some power. He had earlier in life won admiration and prizes for his verse and he later completed a metrical version of the Psalms.

One complaint about his behaviour is that he demanded that people should pray with him in public. Samuel Johnson, who himself knew something of melancholy madness, defended him: 'Although, rationally speaking, it is greater madness not to pray at all than to pray as Smart did, I am afraid there are so many people who do not pray that their understanding is not called in question.' ['Crusions' in the poem are a kind of carp.]

In the playful fire
Ananias, Azarias and Misael

O all ye workes of the Lord, blesse ye the Lorde: prayse hym, and
magnifye hym for ever.

O ye Aungelles of the Lorde, blesse ye the Lorde: prayse ye hym,
and magnifye hym for ever.

O ye heavens, blesse ye the Lorde: prayse hym, and magnifye hym
for ever.

O ye waters that be above the firmament, blesse ye the Lorde:
prayse hym, and magnifye hym for ever.

O all ye powers of the Lorde, blesse ye the Lorde: prayse hym, and
magnifye hym for ever.

O ye Sunne, and Moone, blesse ye the Lorde: prayse hym, and
magnifye hym for ever.

O ye starres of heaven, blesse ye the Lorde: prayse hym, and
magnifye hym for ever.

O ye showres, and dewe, blesse ye the Lorde: prayse him, and
magnifye hym for ever.

O ye wyndes of God, blesse ye the Lorde: prayse him, and magnifye
hym for ever.

O ye fyre and heate, blesse ye the Lorde: prayse hym, and magnifye
hym for ever.

O ye wynter and sommer, blesse ye the Lorde: prayse hym, and
magnifye hym for ever.

O ye dewes and frostes, blesse ye the Lorde: prayse him, and magnifye hym for ever.

O ye froste and colde, blesse ye the Lorde: prayse hym, and magnifye hym for ever.

O ye ice and snowe, blesse ye the Lorde: prayse hym, and magnifye hym for ever.

O ye nyghtes and dayes, blesse ye the Lorde: prayse hym, and magnifye hym for ever.

O ye nyght and darkenesse, blesse ye the Lorde: prayse hym, and magnifye hym for ever.

O ye lighteninges and cloudes, blesse ye the Lorde: prayse hym, and magnifye hym for ever.

O let the earth blesse the Lorde: yes, lette it prayse hym, and magnifye hym for ever.

O ye mountaynes and hylles, blesse ye the Lorde: prayse hym, and magnifye hym for ever.

O all ye grene thinges upon the earth, blesse ye the Lorde: prayse him, and magnifye hym for ever.

O ye welles, blesse ye the Lorde: prayse hym, and magnyfye hym for ever.

O ye seas and fluddes, blesse ye the Lorde: prayse him, and magnyfye him for ever.

O ye whales, and all that move in the waters, blesse ye the Lorde: prayse him, and magnifye hym for ever.

O all ye foules of the ayre, blesse ye the Lorde: prayse hym, and magnifie him for ever.

O all ye beastes and cattell, blesse ye the Lorde: prayse hym, and magnifye hym for ever.

O ye children of men, blesse ye the Lorde: prayse him, and magnifye hym for ever.

O let Israel blesse the Lorde: prayse him, and magnifye hym for ever.

O ye priestes of the Lord, blesse ye the Lorde: prayse hym, and magnifye hym for ever.

O ye servauntes of the Lorde, blesse ye the Lorde: prayse hym, and magnifye hym for ever.

O ye spyrites and soules of the righteous, blesse ye the Lorde: prayse him, and magnifye him for ever.

O ye holye and humble men of hearte, blesse ye the Lorde: prayse him, and magnifye him for ever.

O Ananias, Azarias, and Misael, blesse ye the Lorde: prayse him,
    and magnifye hym for ever.
Glory bee to the father, and to the sonne: and to the holy ghoste.
As it was in the beginning, is nowe, and ever shalbe: worlde
    wythout ende. Amen.

*This Canticle is entitled 'Benedicite omnia opera domini domino' in the Book
of Common Prayer of 1552. The text comes from a part of the book of Daniel
that the Authorized Version consigns to the Apocrypha, in the sense that it
was, as the Thirty-Nine Articles put it, one of those things that 'the Church
doth read for example of life and instruction of manners; but yet doth it not
apply them to establish any doctrine'. Ananias, Azarias and Misael were
known by their Babylonian hosts as Shadrach, Meshach and Abednego.*

God loves me
Frederick William Faber

Why, then, does God love us? We must answer, Because He created
us. This then would make mercy the reason of His love. But why did
He create us? Because He loved us. We are entangled in this circle,
and do not see how to escape from it. But it is a fair prison. We can
rest in it, while we are on earth; and if we are never to know anything
more, then we will make our home in it for eternity. Who would tire
of such captivity? God loves us because He has created us. What sort
of a feeling is it which the peculiarity of having created someone out
of nothing would give us? Who can tell? We suppose it to be a feeling
which contains in itself all the grounds of all earthly loves, such as
paternal, fraternal, conjugal, and filial; and of all angelic loves
besides, of which we know nothing. We suppose it to contain them
all, not only in an infinite degree, but also in the most inconceivably
eminent manner, and further than that, with an adorable simplicity
which belongs only to the divine nature. But when we have imagined
all this, we see that something remains over and above in a Creator's
love, which we cannot explain; but which we must suppose to be a
feeling arising out of His having created us out of nothing, and
which is what it is, because He is what He is, the infinitely blessed

God. This then is our answer. He loves us because He has created us. Certainly the mystery does not fill our minds with light; at least not with such light as we can communicate; but, which is far more, it sets our hearts on fire.

God made me lovable
Thomas Traherne

Had I been alive in Adam's stead, how should I have Admired the
    Glory of the world!
What a Confluence of Thoughts
and Wonders
and Joys
and Thanksgivings would have replenished me
in the sight of so Magnificent a Theatre,
so Bright a Dwelling Place;
so Great a Temple,
so Stately a House
replenished with all Kind of Treasure,
raised out of Nothing,
Created for me and for me alone.
Shall I now Despise them?
When I consider the Heavens which Thou hast made,
the moon and stars which are the Works of thy Fingers;
what is Man that Thou art Mindfull of Him,
or the Son of Man, that Thou Visitest Him!
Thou hast made Him a little lower then the Angels
and Crowned him with Glory and Honour!
O what Love must that needs be, that prepared such a Palace!
Attended with what Power!
With what Wisdom Illuminated!
Abounding with what Zeal!
And how Glorious must the King be, that could out of Nothing
    Erect such a Curious, so Great, and so Beautifull a Fabrick!
It was Glorious while new:
and is as new as it was Glorious.

But this is Small.

What O my Lord could I desire to be which Thou hast not made me!

If Thou hast exprest Thy Love in furnishing the House – How Gloriously doth it Shine in the Possessor!

My Lims and Members when rightly Prized, are Comparable to the fine Gold;

The Topaz of Ethiopia and the Gold of Ophir are not to be compared to them.

What Diamonds are Equal to my Eyes;

What Labyrinths to mine Ears;

What Gates of Ivory, or Rubie Leaves to the Double Portal of my Lips and Teeth? Is not Sight a Jewel?

Is not Hearing a Treasure?

Is not Speech a Glory?

O my Lord, Pardon my Ingratitude and pity my Dulness,

who am not Sensible of these Gifts.

The freedom of thy Bounty hath deceived me.

These things were too near to be considered.

Thou preventedst me with thy Blessings, and I was not aware.

But now I give Thanks and Adore and Praise Thee for these Inestimable favors.

I believe Thou lovest me, because Thou hast endued me, with these Sacred and Living Treasures.

Holy Father, henceforth I more Desire to esteem them, than Palaces of Gold!

Yea tho they were given me by Kings,

I confess unto Thee that I am Richer in them.

O what Joy, what Delight and Jubilee should there always be, would men Prize the Gifts of God according to their Value!

But what Creature could I desire to be which I am not Made?

There are Angels and Cherubim.

I rejoice, O Lord, in their Happiness; and that I am what I am by thy Grace and favor.

Suppose, O my Soul, there were no Creature made at all,

And that GOD making Thee alone offered to make Thee what Thou wouldst.

What couldst Thou Desire; or what wouldst Thou wish, or Crave to be?

Since GOD is the most Glorious of all Beings, and the most
    Blessed,
couldst thou wish any more then to be His IMAGE!
O my Soul, He hath made thee His Image.
Sing, O ye Angel, and Laud His Name ye Cherubims:
Let all the Kingdoms of the Earth be Glad,
and let all the Hosts of Heaven rejoice –
for He hath made His Image, the Likeness of Himself, his own
    Similitude.
What Creature, what Being, what Thing more Glorious could there
    be?
GOD from all Eternity was infinitely Blessed and desired to make
    one infinitely Blessed.
He was infinite LOVE,
and being Lovely in being so,
Would prepare for Himself a most Lovely Object.
Having Studied from all Eternity,
He saw none more Lovely than the Image of His Love, His own
    Similitude.
O Dignity Unmeasurable!
O Exaltation Passing Knowledge!
O Joy Unspeakable!
Triumph, O my Soul and Rejoyce for ever!
I see that I am infinitely Beloved.
For Infinite Love hath exprest and pleased itself in Creating an
    Infinite Object.
GOD is LOVE,
and my Soul is Lovely!
God is Loving, and His Image Amiable.
O my Soul, these are the Foundations of an Eternal Friendship
    between GOD and Thee.
He is infinitely Prone to Love,
and Thou art Like Him.
He is infinitely Lovely
and Thou art Like Him.
What can more Agree than that which is infinitely Lovely, and so
    Prone to love,
What Joys and Affections will be Excited between them!
What infinite Treasures will they be to each other!
O my GOD, Thou hast Glorified thy self,

and thy Creature infinitely,
in making thine Image!
It is fitted for the Throne of GOD!
It is meet to be thy Companion!
It is so Sublime and Wonderfull and Amiable,
that all Angels and Men were Created to Admire it,
As it was Created to Admire Thee,
and to live in Communion with Thee for ever.

*Thomas Traherne (1637–74), a country parson in Herefordshire, wrote short
meditations in groups of a hundred, hence their published name* Centuries
of Meditation. *The meditations here form numbers 65–68 of the* First
Century. *Traherne stressed the affirmative way to God, through strength of
love, and unlike his contemporaries did not start from mankind's sinfulness.
His* Centuries *were not published until the early twentieth century and new
manuscripts, some still unpublished, have been discovered since then. Traherne's repetitive technique is startlingly unlike that of any other writer.*

We seek your face
Alcuin

Eternal Light, shine in our hearts.
Eternal Goodness, deliver us from evil.
Eternal Power, be our support.
Eternal Wisdom, scatter the darkness of our ignorance.
Eternal Pity, have mercy upon us,
That with all our heart and mind and soul and strength we may seek
thy face, and be brought by thine infinite goodness into thy holy
presence. Amen.

*Alcuin (735–804) was an Englishman, from York, but he wrote this prayer,
as he did his poetry, in Latin, a language through which he communicated
with all Europe in his time. The phrase 'seek thy face' would have put his
readers in mind of Psalm 27 (26 in the Vulgate numbering), 'When thou
saidst, Seek ye my face; my heart said unto thee, Thy face, LORD, will I seek.
Hide not thy face far from me; put not thy servant away in anger: thou hast
been my help; leave me not, neither forsake me, O God of my salvation.'*

We praise God to know him
Augustine of Hippo

You are great, O Lord, and greatly to be praised;
great is your power, and your wisdom infinite.
And mankind would praise you;
man, a particle of your creation;
man, that bears about him his mortality, the witness of his sin,
the witness that you resist the proud.
Yet man would praise you;
he, a particle of your creation.
You awake us to delight in your praise;
for you made us for yourself,
and our heart is restless, until it finds rest in you.
Let me know, O Lord, and understand which is first:
to call on you or to praise you?
to know you or to call on you?
For who can call on you without knowing you?
For he who does not know you, may call upon you as other than
    you are.
Or, is it rather that we call on you so that we may know you?
But how shall they call upon him in whom they have not believed?
Or how shall they believe without a preacher?
And they that seek the Lord shall praise him:
for they that seek shall find him,
and they that find shall praise him.
I will seek you, Lord, by calling upon you;
and I will call upon you, believing in you;
for to us you have been preached.
My faith, O Lord, shall call upon you,
for you have given it to me.
By it you have inspired me,
through the Incarnation of your Son,
through the ministry of the Preacher.

Augustine (354–430) began his autobiographical book Confessions *with this prayer. But really the whole book is a dialogue with God.*

My body and soul's praise
Anselm

Let me bless you in all the actions of my life. Let all my frame,
outwardly and inwardly, glorify and bless you.

My salvation, my light, my glory, let my eyes see you, for you have
created them and prepared them to look upon the beauty of
your excellence.

My music, my delight, let my ears bless you, for you have created
them and prepared them to hear the voice of your joyful
salvation.

My sweetness, my refreshment, let my nostrils bless you, for you
have created them and prepared them to take pleasure in the
sweet odour of your ointments.

My praise, my new song, my rejoicing, let my tongue bless and
magnify you, for you have created them and prepared them to
tell forth your wonderful works.

My wisdom, my meditation, my counsel, let my heart adore and
bless you for ever, for you have given it to me and prepared it to
discern your unspeakable mercies.

My life, my happiness, let my soul, sinful though she be, bless you,
for you have created her and prepared her to enjoy your
goodness.

*Anselm (1033–1109) was a Benedictine monk and, from the age of 60,
Archbishop of Canterbury. Though no mean philosopher he was a man of
prayer first. His motto was* Fides quaerens intellectum, *'Faith seeking
understanding'.*

Worthy the winning
Gerard Manley Hopkins

Nothing is so beautiful as spring –
When weeds, in wheels, shoot long and lovely and lush;
Thrush's eggs look little low heavens, and thrush
Through the echoing timber does so rinse and wring
The ear, it strikes like lightnings to hear him sing;

The glassy pear tree leaves and blooms, they brush
The descending blue; that blue is all in a rush
With richness; the racing lambs too have fair their fling.

What is all this juice and all this joy?
A strain of the earth's sweet being in the beginning
In Eden garden. – Have, get, before it cloy,
Before it cloud, Christ, lord, and sour with sinning,
Innocent mind and Mayday in girl and boy,
Most, O maid's child, thy choice and worthy the winning.

Gerard Manley Hopkins (1844–89) had a keen eye for the particularities of nature. His not very numerous poems tack together his insights, which he sometimes called 'epiphanies' before the word became overused, in often contorted syntactical structures. As a priest he sought God conscientiously, and was often racked by his own temperament.

Creator, grant the prize
John Henry Newman

Whom all obey, –
Maker of man! Who from Thy height
Badest the dull earth bring to light
All creeping things, and the fierce might
    Of beasts of prey; –

And the huge make
Of wild or gentler animal,
Springing from nothing at Thy call,
To serve in their due time, and all
    For sinners' sake;

Shield us from ill!
Come it by passion's sudden stress,
Lurk in our mind's habitual dress,
Or through our actions seek to press
    Upon our will.

Vouchsafe the prize
Of sacred joy's perpetual mood,
And service-seeking gratitude,
And love to quell each strife or feud,
  If it arise.

Grant it, O Lord!
To whom, the Father, Only Son,
And Holy Spirit, Three in One,
In heaven and earth all praise be done,
  With one accord.

This hymn for Friday vespers, 'Hominis superne Conditor', *was translated by John Henry Newman (1801–90) as one of a series of English versions of ancient liturgical hymns that he made between 1836 and 1838, while he was Vicar of St Mary's, the University Church at Oxford, and was seeking ways of renewing worship in the Church of England, in what became known as the Oxford Movement.*

3

Speaking with God

Preparation for prayer
Lancelot Andrewes

Times of prayer
Always. (Luke 18:1)
Without ceasing. (1 Thessalonians 5:17)
At all times. (Ephesians 6:18)
Samuel among such as call upon His name; they called upon the
    LORD and he answered them. (Psalm 99:6)
God forbid that I should sin against the Lord in ceasing to pray for
    you and shewing you the good and the right way. (1 Samuel
    12:23)
We will give ourselves continually to prayer and to the ministry of
    the word. (Acts 6:4)
He kneeled upon his knees three times a day, and prayed and gave
    thanks before his God, as he did aforetime. (Daniel 6:10).
In the evening, and morning, and at noon day will I pray, and that
    instantly, and He shall hear my voice. (Psalm 4:17)
Seven times a day do I praise thee (Psalm 99:164):
   1 In the morning, a great while before day. (Mark 1:35)
   2 In the morning watch (Psalm 63:6 – see also Psalm 130:6)
   3 The third hour of the day. (Acts 2:15)
   4 About the sixth hour. (Acts 10:9)
   5 The hour of prayer, the ninth. (Acts 3:1)
   6 The eventide. (Genesis 14:63)
   7 By night. (Psalm 134:1)
At midnight. (Psalm 119:6)

Places of prayer
In all places where I record My Name, I will come to thee, and I
    will bless thee. (Exodus 20:24)
Let Thine eyes be open towards this house night and day, even
    toward the place of which Thou hast said, My Name shall be

there; that Thou mayest hearken unto the prayer which Thy
servant shall make towards this place. (1 Kings 8:29)

Thou that hearest the prayer
unto Thee shall all flesh come.
The fierceness of man shall turn to Thy praise,
and the fierceness of them shalt Thou refrain.
As for me, I will come into Thy house
even upon the multitude of Thy mercy,
and in Thy fear will I worship
toward Thy Holy Temple.
Hear the voice of my humble petitions,
when I cry unto Thee;
when I hold up my hands
towards the mercy seat of Thy Holy Temple.
We wait for Thy loving-kindness, O God,
in the midst of Thy Temple.

1 Among the faithful and in the congregation. (Psalm 111:1)
2 Enter into thy closet, and, when thou hast shut thy door, pray to
  thy Father which is in secret. (Matthew 6:6)
3 They went up into an upper room. (Acts 1:3)
4 He went up upon the housetop to pray. (Acts 10:9)
5 They went up together into the temple. (Acts 3:1)
6 We kneeled down on the shore, and prayed. (Acts 21:5)
7 He went forth over the brook Cedron, where a garden. (John
  18:1)
8 Let them rejoice in their beds. (Psalm 149:5)
9 He departed into a desert place and there prayed. (Mark 1.35)
10 In every place lifting up holy hands without wrath and doubting.
  (1 Timothy 2:8)

Circumstances of prayer
1 Kneeling: *humiliation.*
  He kneeled down and prayed. (Luke 22:41)
  He went a little further, and fell on His face, and prayed.
  (Matthew 26:39)
  My soul is brought low, even unto the dust, my belly cleaveth
  unto the ground.

2 Sinking the head: *shame.*
   Drooping the face. (Ezra 9:6)
3 Smiting the breast. (Luke 17:13): *indignation.*
4 Shuddering (Acts 16:29): *fear.*
5 Groaning (Isaiah 59:11): *sorrow.*
   Clasping of hands.
6 Raising of eyes and hands (Psalm 25:15; 143:6): *vehement desire.*
7 Blows (Psalm 73:14): *revenge.*
   (For Nos 3–7, see 2 Corinthians 7:11.)

These notes come from the Preces Privatae *('Private Prayers'), translated from the Greek by John Henry Newman. Lancelot Andrewes (1555–1626), when Bishop of Winchester, drew up a scheme of prayer for each day of the week. It was written in a little white vellum-covered notebook, two-and-a-half inches by five inches. Shortly before his death, he gave it to his friend William Laud, later Archbishop of Canterbury, beheaded in 1646. It is now kept in the Bodleian Library, Oxford. Andrewes, a man of learning, was intimately familiar with the Greek of the New Testament, in which he couched his biblically connected notes for prayer.*

Met half way

James Montgomery

We perish if we cease from prayer,
O grant us power to pray!
And when to meet thee we prepare,
Lord, meet us by the way.

James Montgomery (1771–1854), the son of a Moravian pastor, and, after a haphazard youth, the editor of a Sheffield newspaper, is remembered as a writer of hymns, but in his time was a successful poet, unafraid to deal with unusual subjects such as the Moravian missionaries in Greenland and organic evolution in his long poem 'The Pelican Island'.

Give ear to our prayers
Book of Common Prayer (1549)

Lord, we beseech thee, give ear to our prayers, and by thy gracious visitation lighten the darkness of our heart, by our Lord Jesus Christ. Amen.

(Collect for the Third Sunday in Advent)

Want more
Thomas Traherne

Infinite Wants Satisfied produce infinite joys;
And, in his Possession of those Joys, are infinite Joys themselves.
The Desire Satisfied is a Tree of Life.
Desire imports some thing absent: and a Need is what is Absent.
GOD was never without this Tree of Life.
He did Desire infinitely – yet He was never without the Fruits of
     this Tree, which are the Joys it produced.
I must lead you out of this, into another World, to learn your
     Wants.
For till you find them you will never be Happy,
Wants themselves being sacred Occasions and Means of Felicitie.

You must Want like a GOD, that you may be Satisfied like GOD.
Were you not made in His Image?
He is infinitely Glorious, because all His Wants and Supplies are at
     the same time in his Nature from Eternity.
He had, and from Eternity he was without all His Treasures.
From Eternity He needed them, and from Eternity He enjoyed
     them.
For all Eternity is at once in Him both the Empty Durations before
     the World was made, and the full ones after.
His Wants are as Lively as His Enjoyments:
And always present with Him.
For His Life is Perfect, and He feels them both.
His Wants put a Lustre upon His Enjoyments,

and make them infinite.
His Enjoyments being infinite Crown his Wants,
and make them Beautiful even to GOD Himself.
His Wants and Enjoyments being always present,
are Delightful to each other,
stable Immutable Perfective of each other,
and Delightfull to Him.
Who being Eternal and Immutable, Enjoyeth all His Wants and
Treasures together.
His Wants never Afflict Him,
His Treasures never Disturb Him.
His Wants always Delight Him,
His Treasures never Cloy Him.
The Sense of His Wants is always as Great, as if his Treasures were
removed:
and as lively upon Him.
The Sense of His Wants, as it Enlargeth His Life, so it infuseth a
Value,
and continual Sweetness into the Treasures He Enjoyeth.

Here, in his First Century of Meditations *(numbers 43 and 44), Traherne
characteristically pursues with energy his theme that to be fully human is to
want things, will them, love them more strongly, just as God loves and enjoys
strongly. He is unusual for his time (1637–74) in picking up the thread of
Aristotelian and high medieval teaching, that virtue is a question of human
flourishing, and that appetite leads us to God as long as it is not distorted from
its goal. Even more unusually, he expresses his insight in highly poetic prose.*

Grant our desires

John Chrysostom

Almighty God, who hast given us grace at this time with one accord
to make our common supplications unto thee; and dost promise,
that when two or three are gathered together in thy Name thou wilt
grant their requests; Fulfil now, O Lord, the desires and petitions of
thy servants, as may be most expedient for them; granting us in this
world knowledge of thy truth, and in the world to come life everlasting. Amen.

From the Book of Common Prayer, the Order for Evening Prayer. St John Chrysostom (347–407) was Bishop of Constantinople and an electrifying preacher. But he was exiled and ill-treated and died somewhere near the Black Sea. He is a doctor of the Church revered by the East and the West.

The First Commandment
Thomas Ken

O Thou, Who only art Jehovah, if Thou be my God, and if I truly love Thee, I can never suffer any creature to be Thy rival, or to share my heart with Thee: I can have no other God, no other love, but only Thee.

[No man can serve two masters: for either he will hate the one, and love the other; or else he will hold to the one, and despise the other. Ye cannot serve God and mammon. Matthew 6:24]

O infinite Goodness, Thou only art amiable; whatever is amiable besides Thee, is no farther amiable than as it bears some impressions on it of Thy amiableness: and therefore all love, all glory, be to Thee alone.

O my God, O my Love, instil into my soul so entire reverential a love of Thee, that I may love nothing but for Thy sake, or in subordination to Thy love.

[And now, Israel, what doth the LORD thy God require of thee, but to fear the LORD thy God, to walk in all his ways, and to love him, and to serve the LORD thy God with all thy heart and with all thy soul. Deuteronomy 10:12]

O Love, give me grace to study Thy knowledge, that the more I know Thee, the more I may love Thee.

[And this is life eternal, that they might know thee the only true God, and Jesus Christ, whom thou hast sent. John 17:3]

O my God, do Thou create in me a steadfast faith in the veracity, a lively hope in the promises, a firm trust in the power, a confident reliance on the goodness, and satisfactory acquiescence in the all-sufficiency of Thee, my Beloved.

[Now faith is the substance of things hoped for, the evidence of things not seen. Hebrews 11:1.

But without faith it is impossible to please him: for he that cometh to God must believe that he is, and that he is a rewarder of them that diligently seek him. Hebrews 11:6.

To an inheritance incorruptible, and undefiled, and that fadeth not away, reserved in heaven for you. 1 Peter 1:4.

And they that know thy name will put their trust in thee: for thou, LORD, hast not forsaken them that seek thee. Psalm 9:10.

Who is this King of glory? The LORD strong and mighty, the LORD mighty in battle. Psalm 24:8.

Truly my soul waiteth upon God: from him cometh my salvation. He only is my rock and my salvation; he is my defence; I shall not be greatly moved. Psalm 62:1–2.

My soul, wait thou only upon God; for my expectation is from him. Psalm 62:5]

O my God, do Thou create in me an ardent desire of Thy Presence, an heavenly delight in the fruition of Thee, my Beloved.

[As the hart panteth after the water brooks, so panteth my soul after thee, O God. Psalm 42:1.

Delight thyself also in the LORD; and he shall give thee the desires of thine heart. Psalm 37:4]

O my God, fill my heart with thanksgiving for the blessings, praise of the excellence, adoration of the majesty, zeal for the glory of Thee, my Beloved.

[I will bless the LORD at all times: his praise shall continually be in my mouth. Psalm 34:1.

Praise ye the LORD: for it is good to sing praises unto our God; for it is pleasant; and praise is comely. Psalm 147:1.

Exalt ye the LORD our God, and worship at his footstool; for he is holy. Psalm 99:5.

Whether therefore ye eat, or drink, or whatsoever ye do, do all to the glory of God. 1 Corinthians 10:31]

O my God, fill my heart with a repentance for offending, with a constant fear of provoking Thee, my Beloved.

[But if the wicked will turn from all his sins that he hath committed, and keep all my statutes, and do that which is lawful and right, he shall surely live, he shall not die. Ezekiel 18:21.

Praise ye the LORD. Blessed is the man that feareth the LORD, that delighteth greatly in his commandments. Psalm 112:1]

O my God, fill my heart with an affective devotion in prayer, and with a profound humility in ascribing all honour to Thee, my Beloved.

[The effectual fervent prayer of a righteous man availeth much. Epistle of St James 5:16.

Not unto us, O LORD, not unto us, but unto thy name give glory, for thy mercy, and for thy truth's sake. Psalm 115:1]

O my God, create in me a sincere obedience to all the commands, a submissive patience under all the chastisements, an absolute resignation to all the disposals of Thee, my Beloved.

[Not every one that saith unto me, Lord, Lord, shall enter into the kingdom of heaven; but he that doeth the will of my Father which is in heaven. Matthew 7:21.

I was dumb, I opened not my mouth; because thou didst it. Psalm 39:9.

And he (Jesus) went a little further, and fell on his face, and prayed, saying, O my Father, if it be possible, let this cup pass from me: nevertheless not as I will, but as thou wilt. Matthew 26:39]

O my God, let Thy all-powerful love abound in my heart, and in the hearts of all that profess Thy Name; that in all these, and in all other possible instances of Thy love, our souls may be continually employed to praise and to love Thee.

[And this I pray, that your love may abound yet more and more in knowledge and in all judgement. Philippians 1:9]

O my God, let me ever be seeking occasions to excite all I can to adore and love Thee.

[O magnify the LORD with me, and let us exalt his name together. Psalm 34:3.

Oh that men would praise the LORD for his goodness, and for his wonderful works to the children of men! Psalm 107:8]

O my God, I renounce and detest, and bewail, as odious and offensive to Thee, as directly opposite to Thy love and to Thy glory: All self-love, and inordinate love of things below.

[For men shall be lovers of their own selves, covetous, boasters, proud, blasphemers, disobedient to parents, unthankful, unholy. 2 Timothy 3:2.

Love not the world, neither the things that are in the world. If any man love the world, the love of the Father is not in him. 1 John 2:15]

All wilful and affected ignorance.

[(Angels) in flaming fire taking vengeance on them that know not God, and that obey not the gospel of our Lord Jesus Christ. 2 Thessalonians 1:8]

All atheism, or having no God, and polytheism, or having more gods than one.

[The fool hath said in his heart, There is no God. Psalm 14:1.

Your fathers have forsaken me, saith the LORD, and have walked after other gods, and have served them, and have worshipped them, and have forsaken me, and have not kept my law. Jeremiah 16:11]

All heresy, apostasy, and infidelity.

[But there were false prophets also among the people, even as there shall be false teachers among you, who privily shall bring in damnable heresies, even denying the Lord that bought them, and bring upon themselves swift destruction. 2 Peter 2:1.

But we are not of them who draw back unto perdition. Hebrews 10:39.

That they all might be damned who believed not the truth, but had pleasure in unrighteousness. 2 Thessalonians 2:12]

All presumption and despair, distrust and carnal security.

[These things hast thou done, and I kept silence; thou thoughtest that I was altogether such a one as thyself: but I will reprove thee, and set them in order before thine eyes. Psalm 50:21.

And he (Judas) cast down the pieces of silver in the temple, and departed, and went and hanged himself. Matthew 27:5.

They believed not in God, and trusted not in his salvation. Psalm 78:22.

Because sentence against an evil work is not executed speedily, therefore the heart of the sons of men is fully set in them to do evil. Ecclesiastes 8:11]

All voluntary humility, and worshipping of angels; reliance on the creature, or recourse to evil spirits.

[Let no man beguile you of your reward in a voluntary humility and worshipping of angels. Colossians 2:18.

Lo, this is the man that made not God his strength; but trusted in the abundance of his riches, and strengthened himself in his wickedness. Psalm 52:7.

And the soul that turneth after such as have familiar spirits, and after wizards, to go a whoring after them, I will even set my face against that soul, and will cut him off from among his people. Leviticus 20:6]

All unthankfulness and irreligion, lukewarmness and indifference.

[For men shall be lovers of their own selves . . . unthankful, unholy. 2 Timothy 3:2.

The wicked, through the pride of his countenance, will not seek after God: God is not in all his thoughts. Psalm 10:4.

I know thy works, that thou art neither cold nor hot: I would thou wert cold or hot. So then because thou art lukewarm, and neither cold nor hot, I will spue thee out of my mouth. Revelation 3:15

And it shall come to pass at that time, that I will search Jerusalem with candles, and punish the men that are settled on their lees: that say in their heart, the LORD will not do good, neither will he do evil. Zephaniah 1:12]

All impenitence and disregard of divine wrath.

[And when he was come near, he beheld the city, and wept over it. Luke 19:41.

And the harp, and the viol, the tabret, and pipe, and wine, are in their feasts: but they regard not the work of the LORD, neither consider the operation of his hands. Isaiah 5:12]

All indevotion and pride, disobedience, impatience and murmuring.

[This people draw near me with their mouth, and with their lips do honour me, but have removed their heart far from me. Isaiah 29:13.

The fear of the LORD is to hate evil: pride, and arrogancy, and the evil way, and the froward mouth, do I hate. Proverbs 8:13.

Unto them that are contentious, and do not obey the truth, but obey unrighteousness – indignation and wrath. Romans 2:8.

Neither murmur ye, as some of them also murmured, and were destroyed of the destroyer. 1 Corinthians 10:10]

All the least tendencies to any of these impieties.

[Incline not my heart to any evil thing. Psalm 141:4]

From all these and the like hateful violations of Thy love, and from that vengeance they justly deserve, O my God, deliver me, and deliver all faithful people.

O my God, I earnestly pray that Thy love may so prevail over our hearts, that we may sadly lament and abhor all these abominations, and may never provoke Thee.

Thomas Ken (1637–1711) in this extract from The Practice of Divine Love *(1685) provides a framework for praying about the first commandment, supporting each consideration with a quotation from Scripture. His demanding ascetical standards might seem discouraging but he balances the rigour of the law with the repeated invocation of his 'beloved', God.*

Quietness
Book of Common Prayer

O God, from whom all holy desires, all good counsels, and all just works do proceed, give unto thy servants that peace which the world cannot give, that both, our hearts may be set to obey thy commandments, and also that by thee we, being defended from the fear of our enemies, may pass our time in rest and quietness; through the merits of Jesus Christ our Saviour. Amen.

(Evensong)

Finding God within
Walter Hilton

What then is heaven to a reasonable soul? Truly nothing else but Jesus God. For if heaven is only that which is above all things, then God alone is heaven to man's soul, for he alone is above the nature of a soul. Then, if a soul can through grace have knowledge of that blessed nature of Jesus, truly he sees heaven, for he sees God. So there are many men who err in understanding some things that are spoken of God, because they do not understand them spiritually.

Holy Scripture says that a soul who wants to find God must lift her inward eye upward, and seek God above herself. Some people who want to put this teaching into practice, understand this word 'above' to signify the setting of one thing above another in place and worthiness, as one planet is above another in situation and worthiness of bodily position. But that is not the case when the word is taken spiritually; for a soul is above every bodily thing, not visibly in location, but in purity and worthiness of nature. In just the same way God is above all bodily and spiritual creatures, not visibly in location, but in the purity and worthiness of his unchangeable blessed nature.

And therefore whoever wants to seek God wisely, and find him, must not run away with his thoughts as if he would climb above the sun, and cleave the firmament, and imagine his majesty to be like to a hundred suns. But he must rather draw down the sun, and all the firmament, and cast it beneath the place where he stands, and put all this, and all physical things too, at nought. And then, if he can, he should think spiritually both of himself and of God also. And if he does so thus, then the soul will see above itself, then will it see into heaven.

In the same way this word 'within' should be understood. It is often said that a soul shall see our Lord 'within' all things and 'within' itself. It is true that our Lord is within all creatures, but not in the way that the kernel is hidden within the nutshell, or as a little bodily thing is contained within a greater. But he is within all creatures, as holding and preserving them in their being, through the subtlety and power of his own blessed nature, and invisible purity.

For just as something which is most precious and clean is laid within wrappings, so it is said metaphorically that the nature of God, which is most precious, most clean, most goodly, most remote from bodily substance, is hidden within all things. So whoever wants to seek God within, must first forget all bodily things, for all such things are on the outside, as with his own body. And he must stop thinking of his own soul, and think on uncreated nature, that is, Jesus, who made him, keeps him alive, preserves him, and gives him reason, memory and the power to love. Jesus God is within him through his power and sovereign subtlety.

Walter Hilton (1343–96), in this extract from The Ladder of Perfection, *is not merely saying that heaven is not 'up there', but that God is not to be found even among our imaginative ideas. Yet he is present within, and, moreover, Jesus, true God as well as man, is there within us, and always to hand.*

Praying for things
Book of Common Prayer

Almighty and everlasting God, who art always more ready to hear than we to pray, and art wont to give more than either we desire or deserve, pour down upon us the abundance of thy mercy, forgiving us those things whereof our conscience is afraid and giving unto us that which our prayer dare not presume to ask; through Jesus Christ our Lord. Amen.

(Collect for the Twelfth Sunday after Trinity)

Inner healing
John Keble

People may find, perhaps, for a time, and very often it is matter of complaint, that they try to attend and cannot; they say the Psalms over with their lips, but their minds are all the while upon their own troubles. Thus they seem to feel to themselves, and they are tempted to say, What good is this worship doing me? But if they persevere they will find, bye and bye, that all the while their wounds have been healing secretly. It may be, their seeming weariness is a trial, by which the enemy is permitted to vex them, and if they resolutely refuse to give way to it, it may cease altogether, and they may find, even in this world, what a joyful and pleasant thing it is to be thankful.

John Keble (1792–1866), though credited with instigating the explosion of activity that became known as the Oxford Movement, remained a country clergyman. His poetry was hugely popular and influential and after his death eleven volumes of his sermons were published. This passage comes from a sermon for the twenty-first Monday after Trinity.

A brisk example
Christopher Smart

For I will consider my Cat Jeoffry.
For he is the servant of the Living God duly and daily serving him.
For at the first glance of the glory of God in the East he worships in
his way.
For this is done by wreathing his body seven times round with
elegant quickness.
For then he leaps up to catch the musk, which is the blessing of
God upon his prayer.
For he rolls upon prank to work it in.
For having done duty and received blessing he begins to consider
himself.
For this he performs in ten degrees.
For first he looks upon his forepaws to see if they are clean.

For secondly he kicks up behind to clear away there.

For thirdly he works it upon stretch with the forepaws extended.

For fourthly he sharpens his paws by wood.

For fifthly he washes himself.

For sixthly he rolls upon wash.

For seventhly he fleas himself, that he may not be interrupted upon the beat.

For eighthly he rubs himself against a post.

For ninthly he looks up for his instructions.

For tenthly he goes in quest of food.

For having consider'd God and himself he will consider his neighbour.

For if he meets another cat he will kiss her in kindness.

For when he takes his prey he plays with it to give it a chance.

For one mouse in seven escapes by his dallying.

For when his day's work is done his business more properly begins.

For he keeps the Lord's watch in the night against the adversary.

For he counteracts the powers of darkness by his electrical skin and glaring eyes.

For he counteracts the Devil, who is death, by brisking about the life.

For in his morning orisons he loves the sun and the sun loves him.

For he is of the tribe of Tiger.

For the Cherub Cat is a term of the Angel Tiger.

For he has the subtlety and hissing of a serpent, which in goodness he suppresses.

For he will not do destruction, if he is well fed, neither will he spit without provocation.

For he purrs in thankfulness, when God tells him he's a good Cat.

For he is an instrument for the children to learn benevolence upon.

For every house is incomplete without him and a blessing is lacking in the spirit.

For the Lord commanded Moses concerning the cats at the departure of the Children of Israel from Egypt.

For every family had one cat at least in the bag.

For the English Cats are the best in Europe.

For he is the cleanest in the use of his forepaws of any quadruped.

For the dexterity of his defence is an instance of the love of God to him exceedingly.

For he is the quickest to his mark of any creature.

For he is tenacious of his point.

For he is a mixture of gravity and waggery.

For he knows that God is his Saviour.

For there is nothing sweeter than his peace when at rest.

For there is nothing brisker than his life when in motion.

For he is of the Lord's poor and so indeed is he called by benevolence perpetually. Poor Jeoffry! poor Jeoffry! the rat has bit thy throat.

For I bless the name of the Lord Jesus that Jeoffry is better.

For the divine spirit comes about his body to sustain it in complete cat.

For his tongue is exceeding pure so that it has in purity what it wants in music.

For he is docile and can learn certain things.

For he can set up with gravity, which is patience upon approbation.

For he can fetch and carry, which is patience in employment.

For he can jump over a stick, which is patience upon proof positive.

For he can spraggle upon waggle at the word of command.

For he can jump from an eminence into his master's bosom.

For he can catch the cork and toss it again.

For he is hated by the hypocrite and miser.

For the former is afraid of detection.

For the latter refuses the charge.

For he camels his back to bear the first notion of business.

For he is good to think on, if a man would express himself neatly.

For he made a great figure in Egypt for his signal services.

For he killed the Ichneumon-rat very pernicious by land.

For his ears are so acute that they sting again.

For from this proceeds the passing quickness of his attention.

For by stroking of him I have found out electricity.

For I perceived God's light about him both wax and fire.

For the Electrical fire is the spiritual substance, which God sends from heaven to sustain the bodies both of man and beast.

For God has blessed him in the variety of his movements.

For, tho he cannot fly, he is an excellent clamberer.

For his motions upon the face of the earth are more than any other quadruped.

For he can tread to all the measures upon the music.

For he can swim for life.

For he can creep.

In this celebrated section from the surviving fragments of the long poem 'Jubi-late Agno', Christopher Smart (1722–71) discerns the worship that his cat gives in a cat-like way to God. Jeoffry looks first to God, then considers himself and his neighbour. He is of God's poor, like the poor of the Old Testament who expected salvation from God. He is blessed by God and acts according to God's will, counteracting the Devil's wiles. At the same time, Smart is contemplat-ing in a human way the blessings of God. Smart was mad at the time, or at least detained on the grounds of madness. But the peculiar private meanings and significances that Smart includes do not vitiate his poetic considerations of his cat Jeoffry, or disqualify him from prayerful reflections.

'Jubilate Agno' was not published until 1939. Benjamin Britten used part of it for his cantata 'Rejoice in the Lamb' (1943).

God's will in me
George MacDonald

I lay last night and knew not why I was sad.
''Tis well with God,' I said, 'and he is the truth;
Let that content me.' – 'Tis not strength, nor youth,
Nor buoyant health, nor a heart merry-mad,
That makes the fact of things wherein men live:
He is the life, and doth my life outgive;
In him there is no gloom, but all is solemn-glad,

I said to myself, 'Lo, I lie in a dream
Of separation, where there comes no sign;
My waking life is hid with Christ in God,
Where all is true and potent-fact divine.'
I will not heed the thing that doth but seem;
I will be quiet as lark upon the sod;
God's will, the seed, shall rest in me the pod.

George MacDonald (1824–1905) found himself rejected as a Congregational minister by his own congregation. He is enthusiastically read today as an author of myths for children and for adults, but in his day his poetry was highly regarded. His Diary of an Old Soul *gives the thoughts of the narra-tor for each day of the year; these are for 6 and 7 December.*

4

Our Father

The Lord's Prayer

Our Father, who art in heaven,
hallowed be thy name;
thy kingdom come:
thy will be done, on earth as it is in heaven.
Give us this day our daily bread;
and forgive us our trespasses,
as we forgive those who trespass against us:
and lead us not into temptation:
but deliver us from evil. Amen.

The Lord's Prayer represents the answer by Jesus to the question recounted in the Gospel according to to Luke; 'And it came to pass, that, as he was praying in a certain place, when he ceased, one of his disciples said unto him, Lord, teach us to pray, as John also taught his disciples' (11:1). Sometimes a devotional 'doxology' is added, 'For thine is the kingdom, the power and the glory, for ever and ever.' As with other very old and familiar prayers, the wording of the Lord's Prayer retains archaisms. The English version became standardized in the reign of Henry VIII. Before that, there was a variety of English versions, though it was also known in Latin even by ordinary country people, as Eamon Duffy explains in his remarkable study of fifteenth- and sixteenth-century society, The Stripping of the Altars.

Seven askings

William Caxton

The mystery of this devout orison, *Pater noster*, is that it containeth seven petitions or askings.

The first is of the eternal goods, that we may have them; and therefore saith he: *Pater noster qui es in coelis, sanctificetur nomen tuum,*

40

that is as much for to say: Father that art reigning in heaven, thy sweet name be blessed.

The second petition is of the goods spiritual that we may receive them and therefore saith he: *Adveniat regnum tuum.* That is to say, May thy realm come to us, whereas we may see thee.

The third petition is: *Fiat voluntas tua sicut in coelo et in terra*, that is to say: Over all be thy will fulfilled and done so that into heaven my soul be led.

The fourth petition is: *Panem nostrum quotidianum da nobis hodie*, and this petition here is demanded of the name of fortune, which is a gift of the Holy Ghost. And the asking is this: Lord give us this day food, so that of thine we may have cure, that is to say that our Lord God will give us our living, so that for lack of it we leave not the service of God, whereof also we may part and deal to the poor folk, members of God.

The fifth petition is: *Et dimitte nobis debita rostra, sicut et nos dimittimus debitoribus nostris*; that is to say; Pardon to us our misdeeds and faults, as we forgive others the misdeeds by them done to us.

The sixth petition is: *Et ne nos inducas in tentationem.* That is to say, And lead us not into temptation. And here is to be known that we be tempted principally of three things, the first is God, for to approve our power, secondly our flesh, for to have our appetite and lust, thirdly is the enemy for to deceive us. Of the first saith our Lord: *Beatus vir qui suffert tentationem*, etc., Blessed is he that suffereth temptation in the tribulation that God sendeth, for if he be approved, in heaven he shall be crowned. Of the second temptation speaketh S. James and saith: *Unusquisque vero tentatur a concupiscentia sua*, etc. Every one is oft tempted for to pursue his desires. Of the third saith the Scripture: *Sathanas temptavit cor tuum*, etc., Satan hath made thee to fall in villainy.

The seventh petition is: *Sed libera nos a malo*, that is as much for to say: Deliver us from all evil that letteth us for to love thee. After followeth: *Amen, hoc est fiat*, that is to say: The petitions before demanded be confirmed and granted.

William Caxton (1415–92) was an editor and publisher as much as a printer. In 1483 he printed The Golden Legend, *by Jacobus de Voragine (1275), which had long been immensely popular. It contained not only saints' lives but also expositions of the Creed, the Commandments and the Mass. The 'considerations on the Lord's Prayer' are no more than notes that a preacher might use to put meat on in Sunday homilies. The quotation* 'Beatus vir . . .' *comes from the Epistle of St James (1:12), and* 'Sat[h]anas temptavit' *from the Acts of the Apostles (5:3).*

In heaven and my heart
Girolamo Savonarola

Who art in heaven

O Lord God, our Almighty Father; I know that you are everywhere by your essence; you have by your own power created all things, and are present in all, preserving them that they may not fall back into nothing. You are truly everywhere, you see all things, nothing can escape your sight, the darkness shall not be dark to you, and night shall be as light as day (Psalm 138:12).

You are present everywhere in your power, for your might penetrates all things. You work all in all (1 Corinthians, 12:6) and in your strength you govern all things.

I have no need to seek you further than in my own heart. Whither shall I go from your spirit? Or whither shall I flee from your face? If I ascend into heaven, you are there: if I descend into hell, you are present. If I take my wings early in the morning and dwell in the uttermost parts of the sea, even there also shall your hand lead me, and your right hand shall hold me (Psalm 138:7).

In what sense then do I say, O Lord God, 'Who art in heaven'? Are you not also on earth? It must needs be that you dwelt in heaven otherwise than on earth. In heaven are the angels and the blessed, who form the heaven of heavens, and you dwell in them in such unspeakable fullness, that you seem not to be in other creatures, for these are mere nothings in comparison with the blessed hierarchies of heaven. Heaven is made up also of the saints, who are raised above earthly things, and are pure, simple, full of divine light, and free from stain, and their conversation is always in heaven.

In them you dwell by your grace, which is of such priceless worth, that he who has it not has nothing, though he possess the whole world beside. You are in all these heavens in virtue of your unspeakable goodness and mercy; and, O Lord God, our Father, you bid us say, 'Who art in heaven', so that we may lift up our thoughts to the heavenly kingdom, and put aside all earthly affections, remembering that we ought to desire nothing here below, for we say that you are in heaven and not 'on earth'.

Heaven is your throne and the earth your footstool (Isaiah 66:1). With much confidence, therefore, we will ask of you gifts great as well as small, for you are a mighty Father, abounding in all riches, and possessing all heavenly treasures. For eye has not seen, nor ear heard, neither has it entered into the heart of man to conceive what things God has prepared for them that love Him (1 Corinthians 2:9).

Girolamo Savonarola (1452–1498) published his commentary On the Lord's Prayer *in 1495. As a Dominican Friar he lived in the friary of San Marco at Florence (now a museum), where Fra Angelico had painted his wonderful series of murals. After the overthrow of the Medicis, Savonarola's preaching against vice and frivolity was influential in the new democratic republic enacting stern laws. He denounced the abuses of churchmen and gained the enmity of Pope Alexander VI, who accused him of heresy. He was excommunicated, tried, hanged and burnt. By 1996 the injustice done to Savonarola was so far recognized that official steps were under way for his beatification by the Church.*

(The psalm he quotes is numbered 139 in the Authorized Version.)

On earth as in heaven
Thomas Traherne

You never Enjoy the World aright,
till you see how a Sand Exhibiteth the Wisdom and Power of God:
And Prize in every Thing the service which they do you,
by Manifesting His Glory and Goodness to your Soul, far more than
    the Visible Beauty on their Surface,
or the Material Services, they can do your Body.
Wine by its Moysture quencheth my Thirst, whether I consider it or
    not:
but to see it flowing from his Love who gave it unto Man,
    Quencheth the Thirst even of the Holy Angels.
To consider it, is to Drink it Spiritually.
To Rejoice in its Diffusion is to be of a Publick Mind.

And to take Pleasure in all the Benefits it doth to all is Heavenly –
for so they do in Heaven.
To do so, is to be Divine and Good –
and to imitate our Infinite and Eternal Father.

Your Enjoyment of the World is never right,
till every Morning you awake in Heaven:
see your self in your father's Palace:
and look upon the Skies and the Earth and the Air, as Celestial
    Joys:
having such a Reverend Esteem of all, as if you were among the
    Angels.
The Bride of a Monarch, in her Husband's Chamber, hath no such
    Causes of Delight as you.

You never Enjoy the World aright,
till the Sea it self floweth in your Veins,
till you are Clothed with the Heavens,
and Crowned with the Stars,
and perceive your self to be the Sole Heir of the whole World:
and more than so, because Men are in it who are every one Sole
    Heirs, as well as you.
Till you can Sing and Rejoyce and Delight in GOD, as Misers do in
    Gold,
and Kings in Scepters,
you never Enjoy the World.

Till your Spirit filleth the whole World,
and the Stars are your Jewels,
till you are as Familiar with the Ways of God in all Ages
as with your Walk and Table:
till you are intimately Acquainted with that Shady Nothing out of
    which the World was made:
till you love Men so as to Desire their Happiness, with a Thirst
    equal to the zeal of your own:
till you Delight in GOD for being Good to all:
you never Enjoy the World.
Till you more feel it than your Private Estate,
and are more present in the Hemisphere, considering the Glories
    and the Beauties there, than in your own House.

Till you remember how lately you were made,
and how wonderfull it was when you came into it:
and more rejoice in the Palace of your Glory,
than if it had been made but to-Day Morning.

Yet further, you never Enjoy the World aright,
till you so love the Beauty of Enjoying it,
that you are Covetous and Earnest to Persuade others to Enjoy it.
And so perfectly hate the Abominable Corruption of Men in
    Despising it,
that you had rather suffer the flames of Hell then willingly be
    Guilty of their Error.
There is so much Blindness, and Ingratitude, and Damned folly
    in it.
The World is a Mirror of infinite Beauty,
yet no man sees it.
It is a Temple of Majesty
yet no Man regards it.
It is a Region of Light and Peace,
did not Men Disquiet it.
It is the Paradise of God.
It is more to Man since he is fal'n, than it was before.
It is the Place of Angels,
and the Gate of Heaven.
When Jacob walked out of His Dream, he said,
God is here and I wist it not. How Dreadful is this place! This is
    none other, than the House of God, and the Gate of Heaven.

Thomas Traherne (1637–74), from the First Century of Meditations,
numbers 27–31.

Debitoribus nostris
John Kettlewell

O Almighty Lord, Father of mercies, let the sight of my necessities
move the hearts of my Creditors to have mercy on me, and let their
own infinite greater sums which they stand indebted in to Thee,
prompt them to show compassion to and have patience with me, as

they expect mercy themselves from Thee. And make me like willing to do justice to them all, to the utmost of that worldly estate I have to dispose of; cheerfully trusting to the protection of Thy good providence, and choosing rather to want the necessaries of life, than the innocence thereof.

Those who have kindly forgiven me what I cannot pay, do Thou, O Lord, bless and reward, and make it up abundantly to them by Thy good providence.

And, O righteous and merciful Lord, forgive me my worst debts, my sins, which are many and grievous, and cleanse me from the guilt of them, that I may not be arraigned for them at Thy dreadful tribunal.

Grant this, O Lord, through the merits and satisfaction of my blessed Lord and Saviour Jesus Christ. Amen.

We say 'as we forgive those who trespass against us', though the words in the Gospel according to St Luke, in the translation of the Authorized Version, are, 'for we also forgive every one that is indebted to us'. When people were imprisoned for debt, the metaphor had more power. John Kettlewell (1653–95), who wrote this prayer for debtors, was a clergyman deprived of his living because he could not in conscience acknowledge the new king when James II was deposed in 1688. Kettlewell's devotional writings include A Companion for the Penitent *and* Persons Troubled in Mind *(1694) and the optimistic* Death Made Comfortable, *published in 1695, the year of his own death. The prayer here was included in what to us sounds the amusingly entitled* Churchman's Companion in the Closet *(1858).*

PART TWO

God with Us

God becomes man

Come, Emmanuel
J. M. Neale

O come, O come, Emmanuel,
And ransom captive Israel,
That mourns in lonely exile here,
Until the Son of God appear.
Rejoice! Rejoice! Emmanuel
Shall come to thee, O Israel.

O come, Thou Rod of Jesse, free
Thine own from Satan's tyranny;
From depths of Hell Thy people save,
And give them victory o'er the grave.
Rejoice! Rejoice! Emmanuel
Shall come to thee, O Israel.

O come, Thou Dayspring, come and cheer
Our spirits by Thine advent here;
Disperse the gloomy clouds of night,
And death's dark shadows put to flight.
Rejoice! Rejoice! Emmanuel
Shall come to thee, O Israel.

O come, Thou Key of David, come,
And open wide our heavenly home;
Make safe the way that leads on high,
And close the path to misery.
Rejoice! Rejoice! Emmanuel
Shall come to thee, O Israel.

O come, O come, Thou Lord of Might,
Who to Thy tribes, on Sinai's height,
In ancient times did'st give the Law,
In cloud, and majesty and awe.
Rejoice! Rejoice! Emmanuel
Shall come to thee, O Israel.

The original Latin hymn, of which this is a translation by J. M. Neale (1818–66), was a versification of the five great antiphons – each beginning with a vocative 'O' – for the days before Christmas. They are of ancient origin, from the sixth or seventh centuries, and were recited with the Magnificat at evensong. The text here appeared in the first edition of Hymns Ancient and Modern *in 1861.*

Wake up
John Henry Newman

Hark, a joyful voice is thrilling,
    And each dim and winding way
Of the ancient Temple filling;
    Dreams, depart! for it is day.

Christ is coming! – From thy bed,
    Earth-bound soul, awake and spring –
With the sun new-risen to shed
    Health on human suffering.

Lo! to grant a pardon free,
    Comes a willing Lamb from Heaven;
Sad and tearful, hasten we,
    One and all, to be forgiven.

Once again He comes in light,
    Girding earth with fear and woe;
Lord! be Thou our loving Might,
    From our guilt and ghostly foe.

To the Father, and the Son,
And the Spirit, who in Heaven
Ever witness, Three and One,
Praise on earth be ever given.

This is a translation by John Henry Newman (1801–90) of an Advent hymn, En clara vox redarguit, *from the breviary. It connects the coming of Christ at Christmas with his second coming at the end of the world.*

Word made flesh
The Angelus

The Angel of the Lord declared unto Mary.
Response: And she conceived of the Holy Spirit.
Hail, Mary, full of grace, the Lord is with thee. Blessed art thou among women, and blessed is the fruit of thy womb, Jesus. Holy Mary, Mother of God, pray for us sinners, now, and at the hour of our death. Amen.

Behold the handmaid of the Lord.
Response: Be it done unto me according to thy word.
Hail, Mary, full of grace, the Lord is with thee. Blessed art thou among women, and blessed is the fruit of thy womb, Jesus. Holy Mary, Mother of God, pray for us sinners, now, and at the hour of our death. Amen.

And the Word was made Flesh.
Response: And dwelt among us.
Hail, Mary, full of grace, the Lord is with thee. Blessed art thou among women, and blessed is the fruit of thy womb, Jesus. Holy Mary, Mother of God, pray for us sinners, now, and at the hour of our death. Amen.

Pray for us, O holy Mother of God.
Response: That we may be made worthy of the promises of Christ.

Let us pray. Pour forth, we beseech thee, O Lord, thy grace into our hearts, that we to whom the Incarnation of Christ thy Son was made known by the message of an angel, may by his Passion and Cross be brought to the glory of his Resurrection. Through the same Christ Our Lord. Amen.

The recitation of the prayer 'Hail Mary' in the evening seems to have originated in the thirteenth century. Later the Angelus, as it became known, was said in the early morning and at noon too. The Hail Mary itself is composed of two verses from the Gospel according to St Luke (1:28 and 1:42), with a concluding request for intercession by the Mother of God (Theotokos, as the Universal Council of Eastern and Western bishops at Ephesus called Mary in 431).

Midnight sun
Giles Fletcher

Who can forget, never to be forgot,
The time when all the world in slumber lies,
When, like the stars, the singing Angels shot
To earth, and heaven awaked all his eyes
To see another Sun at midnight rise.
   On earth was never sight of pareil fame:
   For God before man like himself did frame,
But God himself now like mortal man became.

A child he was, and had not learnt to speak,
That with his word the world before did make;
His mother's arms him bore, he was so weak,
That with one hand the vaults of heaven could shake.
See how small room my infant Lord doth take,
   Whom all the world is not enough to hold.
   Who of his years or of his age hath told?
Never such age so young, never a child so old.

From Christ's Victorie, and Triumph in Heaven, and Earth, over, and after Death *(1610) by Giles Fletcher (1586–1623). Giles Fletcher and his brother Phineas were described 100 years ago as 'curious, half-diseased, half-divine poets', but Giles's own long poem, though split into four parts of quite different technique, was attempted as an epic in the fashion of Du Bartas' 'Divine Weeks and Works', translated into English in 1605 by Joshua Sylvester. No one, really, now reads Du Bartas, even in English, and Fletcher is read even less.*

What the shepherds saw
John Byrom

To Bethlehem straight th'enlightened shepherds ran,
To see the wonder God had wrought for man;
And found, with Joseph and the blessed Maid,
Her Son, the Saviour, in a manger laid.
Amazed, the wondrous story they proclaim,
The first apostles of his infant fame.

From 'A Hymn for Christmas Day' by John Byrom (1692–1763), poet and contriver of shorthand.

The Nativitie of Christ
Robert Southwell

Beholde the father, is his daughter's sonne:
The bird that built the nest, is hatched therein:
The olde of yeares, an houre hath not out runne:
Eternall life, to live doth now beginne.
The word is dumme: the mirth of heaven doth weepe:
Might feeble is: and force doth faintly creepe.
O dying soules, beholde your living spring:
O dasled eyes, beholde your sonne of grace:
Dull eares, attend what word this word doth bring:
Up heavie hartes: with joye your joye embrace.
From death, from darke, from deafenesse, from dispaires:
This life, this light, this word, this joy repaires.

Gift better then himselfe, God doth not know:
Gift better then his God, no man can see:
This gift doth here the gever geven bestow:
Gift to this gift let each receiver bee.
God is my gift, himselfe he freely gave me:
Gods gift am I, and none but God shall have me.
Man altered was by sinne from man to beast:
Beastes foode is haye, haye is all mortall flesh:
Now God is flesh, and lies in Manger prest:
As haye, the brutest sinner to refresh.
O happie fielde wherein this fodder grew,
Whose tast, doth us from beasts to men renew.

Robert Southwell (1561–95) was a Norfolk boy, his father having a house at Horsham St Faith. Robert went to school at Douai, where he could receive a Catholic education, and then joined the Society of Jesus, being ordained a priest and returning to England in 1586, to minister as a priest. He was arrested in 1592, and tortured ten times. After years of solitary confinement he was hanged, drawn and quartered. His poetry, including his best-known poem 'The Burning Babe', was admired in his lifetime and in the early seventeenth century, when an appetite for metaphysical conceits was at its height. In the past century a wider readership has come to realize just how good they really are.

Wonderful exchange
The Missal

O wonderful exchange, the Creator of the human race, taking upon Himself a body and a soul, has vouchsafed to be born of a Virgin, and, appearing here below as man with no earthly father, has made us partakers of His Divinity.

O admirabile commercium: Creator generis humani animatum corpus sumens, de virgine nasci dignatus est, et procedens homo sine semine largitus est nobis suam deitatem.

This antiphon for the Octave of Christmas is familiar in its Latin version from its setting by Giovanni Pierluigi de Palestrina (1525–94).

Sharing in Divinity
Columba Marmion

Now what is the intimate grace of the mystery of the Nativity? What is the fruit that we ought to gather from the contemplation of the Christ Child?

The Church herself indicates this at the first Mass for Christmas Day, that of midnight. After having offered the bread and wine which, in a few moments, are to be changed, by the consecration, into the Body and Blood of Jesus Christ, she sums up her desires in this prayer: 'Grant, O Lord, that the oblation which we offer in today's festival may be acceptable unto Thee, and, by Thy grace, through this most sacred and holy intercourse, may we be found like unto Him in Whom is our substance united to Thee.'

We ask to be partakers of that divinity to which our humanity is united. It is like an exchange. God, in becoming incarnate, takes our human nature and gives us, in return, a participation in His Divine nature.

This thought, so concise in its form, is more explicitly expressed in the secret of the second Mass for Christmas Day: 'Grant, O Lord, that our offerings may be conformed to the mysteries of this day's Nativity, that as He Who is born as man is also God made manifest, so this earthly substance (which He unites to Himself) may confer upon us that which is divine.'

To be made partakers of the Divinity to which our humanity was united in the Person of Christ, and to receive this Divine gift through this humanity itself, such is the grace attached to the celebration of today's mystery.

Our offerings will be 'conformed to the mysteries of this day's Nativity', according to the words of the above quoted prayer, if 'by the contemplation of the Divine work at Bethlehem and the reception of the Eucharistic Sacrament', we participate in the eternal life that Christ wills to communicate to us by His Humanity.

'O admirable exchange,' we shall sing on the octave day, 'the Creator of the human race, taking upon Himself a body and a soul, has vouchsafed to be born of a Virgin, and, appearing here below as man, has made us partakers of His Divinity.'

From Christ in His Mysteries *(1919) by Dom Columba Marmion (1858–1923). The author was born in Dublin and in 1886 entered the Benedictine abbey at Maredsous, Belgium, becoming Abbot in 1909. He had a reputation for holiness.*

Triple epiphany
Liturgy of the Hours

We honour this holy day,
adorned with three miracles:
today the star led the Magi to the manger;
today water was turned into wine for the wedding;
today Christ desired to be baptised in the Jordan,
that he might save us all.
This is the day that the Lord has made;
let us rejoice and be glad in it.
Alleluia.

Antiphon at the Magnificat for Vespers of the Epiphany. The form of this ancient prayer is said to show Greek influence.

Giving to God
Christina Rossetti

11 January
Example kindles enthusiasm, enthusiasm aspires to emulate.

But unfortunately pseudo-aspiration often selects points impossible to be emulated, and overlooks at least some one point within the boundary of possible imitation.

How great a dignity, how great a happiness, to have been one of the Magi!

This, however, we cannot be. Our Saviour no longer dwells in a small humble house, ready to be worshipped with men's hands as though He needed anything.

Neither does any star traverse heaven as our guide. Neither does any dream enable us to mock the counsels of a king.

Nevertheless as those Wise Men offered their treasures to the Visible Presence, so can we offer ours to the Invisible.

Not frankincense or myrrh, necessarily: nay, nor gold either, necessarily.

Yet such as they are, our treasures.

And though not to Christ Whom mortal eyes can look upon, yet as truly to Christ unseen in His Temple or veiled in His poor.

If not gold, then silver; if not silver, then copper.

Yet if our hearts were set on reproducing the Magi in some one particular, I suppose many of us could find gold (though it were only the least gold coin) for our Epiphany offering.

Perhaps many have tried to do so and have succeeded.

Perhaps not one has tried to do so and has failed.

From Time Flies: A Reading Diary *(1885) by Christina Rossetti (1830–94), an uncomfortable writer, who indeed lived an uncomfortable life among unreliable Pre-Raphaelites and aged aunts, often in sickness and often beset by scruples.*

Life of Jesus

Book of Common Prayer

By the mystery of thy holy Incarnation; by thy holy Nativity and Circumcision; by thy Baptism, Fasting, and Temptation,
Good Lord, deliver us.

This prayer comes in the Litany, directed to be sung or said after morning prayer on Sundays, Wednesdays and Fridays.

To take God's side

Frederick William Faber

He apparently consults our interests rather than His own, by making in reality the last identical with the first.

His first thought for sinners is to make repentance easy and light, and strange indeed are the things to which His wisdom can persuade His justice, or His goodness bend His sanctity.

By His own order our liberty seems to take precedence of His law, while the whole of creation is apparently disposed for the convenience of our salvation.

The increase of this love depends upon ourselves.

On this side the grave we can have it when we will, and there is always grace to enable us to ask it and to will it.

The more we ask the more He will give, and reckon the obligation to be on His side rather than on ours.

All that is wanted of us is, to take God's side, to love what He loves, to hate what He hates, and, to sum up all in one word, to belong to Jesus Christ.

From The Creator and the Creature *(1858), a characteristic devotional work of Frederick William Faber (1814–63), the founder of the Brompton Oratory, in which he encourages his readers to embrace the easiness of accepting God's salvation.*

6

Cross and resurrection

The paschal mysteries
Book of Common Prayer

By thine Agony and Bloody Sweat; by thy Cross and Passion; by thy precious Death and Burial; by thy glorious Resurrection and Ascension, and by the Coming of the Holy Ghost,
  Good Lord, deliver us.

(From the Litany)

Agony in the Garden
Ronald Knox

And he came out, and went, as he was wont, to the Mount of Olives; and his disciples also followed him. And when he was at the place, he said unto them, Pray that ye enter not into temptation. And he was withdrawn from them about a stone's cast, and kneeled down, and prayed, saying, Father, if thou be willing, remove this cup from me: nevertheless not my will, but thine, be done. (The Gospel according to St Luke, 22:39)

It is not a question of what I will, but of what thou wilt. Whether I will it or not, is not the point; the point is, Does my Father will it, or no? That is the interpretation we must keep in mind, if we are to understand the theology of the Agony; it is not a conflict between the Will of Jesus and the Will of God, from which the latter emerges successful, it is the Will of Jesus passing beyond itself, being universalised into the Will of God.

A great deal of very loose doctrine is preached on this text: you will find it suggested, for example, that it was the human Will of Jesus of Nazareth which willed to live, and then the divine Will, which he possessed as the Eternal Word of God, came in to correct it. That is theological heresy and psychological nonsense. It is true, of course, that there is in our animal nature an instinct for self-preservation, which some have called the Will to Live. No doubt that repugnance of nature to the idea of death, which tugs a little at the resolution of the bravest of earthly heroes, was operative in the Sacred Humanity of Jesus, and formed a background of horror to the mental Passion of Gethsemane. But that is an instinct, not a will; the Will of Jesus, as a function of the soul, was at that moment, as at every other moment in his life on earth, perfectly in accord with that of his Father. Jesus did not will the Crucifixion, did not will that Judas should betray, Caiaphas conspire against, and Pilate misjudge him – nor did the Father. God never wills what is evil. The Father did will the Passion, did will that Jesus should receive the kiss, stand before the tribunal, tread the way of the Cross, without complaining – so did Jesus. Jesus always willed what was good.

The prayer of Jesus in the Garden of Gethsemane is a pattern for prayer which asks for things in this life. Jesus, as a man, was asking for things from God, as he had asked for things when he performed his miracles, such as the turning of water into wine at Cana or the raising of his friend Lazarus from the dead. The extract here is from a little book published by the Society of SS Peter and Paul, an Anglican society, under the title Bread or Stone: Four Conferences on Impetrative Prayer *by Ronald Knox (1888–1957), at that time (1915) Fellow and Chaplain of Trinity College, Oxford. He must have been confident that his audience would know that impetrative prayer is prayer of request or entreaty.*

The world's life

Alcuin

Dying for the world, here hung the world's life.
Cleansing all by that deadly stream of blood.
When you bowed your head, you raised the world higher
    than the stars,
And, wonder of all time, your death created life.

Alcuin (735–804) went as a boy to the cathedral school at York, of which, aged 43, he became the head. In 782 he went to Aachen to organize the renaissance in learning envisaged by Charlemagne. Fourteen successful years later he retired from the palace school to become Abbot of St Martin's monastery, Tours, living another eight years. His influence on the liturgy of the Church was immense and remains to this day. He wrote his poetry in Latin.

Our sins nailed
Orthodox Liturgy of the Hours

Rejoice you heavens, sound the trumpet foundations of the earth, shout aloud you mountains; for see, Emmanuel has nailed our sins to the Cross, and he who gives life has slain death and raised up Adam, as he loves mankind.

From the stichera of Anatolios used in Great Vespers of the Orthodox Church.

The most peculiar thing
Thomas Traherne

The Cross is the Abyss of Wonders,
the Centre of Desires,
the Schole of Virtues,
the House of Wisdom,
the Throne of Love,
the Theatre of Joys
and the Place of Sorrows;
It is the Root of Happiness,
and the Gate of Heaven.

Of all the Things in Heaven and Earth it is the most Peculiar.
It is the most Exalted of all Objects.
It is an Ensign lifted up for all Nations,
to it shall the Gentiles seek,
His Rest shall be Glorious:
the Dispersed of Judah shall be gathered together to it, from
    the four Corners of the Earth.

If Love be the Weight of the Soul,
and its Object the Centre –
All Eyes and Hearts may convert and turn unto this Object:
cleave unto this Centre,
and by it enter into Rest.
There we might see all Nations Assembled with their Eyes and
    Hearts upon it.
There we may see God's Goodness Wisdom and Power:
yea his Mercy and Anger displayed.
There we may see Man's Sin and infinite value.
His Hope and Fear,
his Misery and Happiness.
There we might see the Rock of Ages,
and the Joys of Heaven.
There we may see a Man Loving all the World,
and a God Dying for Mankind.
There we may see all Types and Ceremonies,
figures and Prophesies.
And all Kingdoms Adoring a Malefactor:
an Innocent Malefactor, yet the Greatest in the World.
There we may see the most Distant Things in Eternity united:
all Mysteries at once couched together and Explained.
The only reason why this Glorious Object is so Publickly
    Admired by Churches and Kingdoms,
and so little thought of by Particular men,
is because it is truly the most Glorious.
It is the Root of Comforts,
and the Fountain of Joys.
It is the only Supreme and Soveraign Spectacle in all Worlds.
It is a Well of Life beneath
in which we may see the face of Heaven above:
and the only Mirror wherein all things appear in their Proper
    Colours –
that is, sprinkled in the Blood of our Lord and Saviour.

The Cross of Christ is the Jacob's ladder
by which we Ascend into the Highest Heavens.
There we see Joyfull Patriarchs,
Expecting Saints,
and Prophets Ministering.

Apostles Publishing
and Doctors Teaching.
All Nations concentering,
and Angels Praising.
That Cross is a Tree set on fire with invisible flame,
that Illuminateth all the World.
The Flame is Love.
The Love in his Bosom who died on it.

These are the fifty-eighth, fifty-ninth and sixtieth in the First Century of
Meditations *by Thomas Traherne (1637–74).*

Tree of life

Venantius Fortunatus

Pange, lingua, gloriosi
proelium certaminis,
et super Crucis trophaeo
dic triumphum nobilem,
qualiter Redemptor orbis
immolatus vicerit.

Sing, my tongue,
The Saviour's glory;
Tell his triumph far and wide;
Tell aloud the famous story
Of his body crucified;
How upon the cross a victim,
Vanquishing in death, he died.

De parentis protoplasti
fraude Factor condolens,
quando pomi noxialis
morte morsu corruit,
ipse lignum tunc notavit,
damna ligni ut solveret.

Eating of the tree forbidden,
Man had sunk in Satan's snare,
When our pitying Creator did
This second tree prepare;
Destined, many ages later,
That first evil to repair.

Crux fidelis,
inter omnes
arbor una nobilis;
nulla talem silva profert,
flore, fronde, germine.
Dulce lignum, dulci clavo,
dulce pondus sustinens!

Faithful Cross!
Above all other,
One and only noble Tree!
None in foliage, none in blossom,
None in fruit thy peers may be;
Sweetest wood and sweetest iron!
Sweetest Weight is hung on thee!

The hymn by Venantius Fortunatus (530–609) from which this extract is taken was written for the procession that brought a part of the true Cross to Queen Radegund in 570. It is now sung as part of the Good Friday devotions.

Venantius supposes for the purpose of the hymn that the cross on which Jesus (the second Adam) died was made from the wood grown from a cutting of that tree from which bore the fruit that brought death to Adam and Eve.

The English translation is by Edward Caswall (1814–78).

Second Adam

John Henry Newman

Fifth Choir of Angelicals:

Praise to the Holiest in the height
    And in the depth be praise:
In all His words most wonderful;
    Most sure in all His ways!

O loving wisdom of our God!
    When all was sin and shame,
A second Adam to the fight
    And to the rescue came.

O wisest love! that flesh and blood
    Which did in Adam fail,
Should strive afresh against the foe,
    Should strive and should prevail;

And that a higher gift than grace
    Should flesh and blood refine,
God's Presence and His very Self,
    And Essence all-divine.

O generous love! that He who smote
    In man for man the foe,
The double agony in man
    For man should undergo;

And in the garden secretly,
    And on the cross on high,
Should teach His brethren and inspire
    To suffer and to die.

This song from The Dream of Gerontius *by John Henry Newman (1801–90) is now used as a popular congregational hymn in church.*

The Passion Chorale
Henry Baker

O sacred head, surrounded
By crown of piercing thorn!
O bleeding head, so wounded,
Reviled and put to scorn!
Our sins have marred the glory
Of thy most holy face,
Yet angel hosts adore thee
And tremble as they gaze.

I see thy strength and vigour
All fading in the strife,
And death with cruel rigor,
Bereaving thee of life;
O agony and dying!
O love to sinners free!
Jesus, all grace supplying,
O turn thy face on me.

In this thy bitter passion,
Good Shepherd, think of me
With thy most sweet compassion,
Unworthy though I be:
Beneath thy cross abiding
For ever would I rest,
In thy dear love confiding,
And with thy presence blest.

*The original Latin poem of which this is a translation has been attributed to
St Bernard, though it seems to be a later work. The first stanza went:*

> *Salve caput cruentatum*
> *totum spinis coronatum*
> *conquassatum vulneratum*
> *harundine verberatum*
> *facie sputis illita.*

The translation here is by Sir Henry Baker (1821–77), and it appeared in the first edition of Hymns Ancient and Modern *in 1864. A German translation had appeared in the seventeenth century. Both versions were sung to a tune by H. L. Hassler published in 1601. This tune became known as the 'Passion Chorale' because it was used by J. S. Bach five times, in his St Matthew Passion. A different version of the English words appears in the* Methodist Hymnal.

Empathy

Anselm

Father adorable and terrible, worthy of worship and of fear, I bless
   you,
whom I have loved, whom I have sought, whom I have ever desired.
My God, my lover, I thirst after you, I hunger for you, I pour out
   my supplications
to you, with all the groanings of my heart I crave for you.
Even as a mother, when her only son is taken from her, sits weeping
   and lamenting
continually beside his sepulchre, even so I also, as I can, not as I
   ought,
having in mind your passion, your buffetings, your scourgings, your
   wounds,
remembering how you were slain for my sake, how you were
   buried,
sit with Mary at the sepulchre in my heart, weeping.
Where faith has laid you, hope seeks to find you, love to anoint
   you. Most gracious, most excellent, most sweet, who will bring
   me to find you outside the sepulchre to wash your wounds with
   my tears, even the marks of the nails.
You daughters of Jerusalem, tell my Beloved that I am sick of love.
Let him show himself to me, let him make himself known unto me.
Let him call me by my name; let him give me rest from my sorrow.

Anselm (1033–1109) was a philosopher who sought understanding through faith. He was an Archbishop of Canterbury who had repeated troubles with secular powers. He wrote an influential though sometimes misunderstood treatise on the atonement, Jesus's sacrificial death. In this prayer he shows that

*men in the eleventh century were as capable of religious feeling as the audi-
ences of Bach's St Matthew Passion, for example, or nineteenth-century con-
templators of the Stations of the Cross.*

Sword of sorrow
Jacopone da Todi

*Stabat Mater dolorosa
juxta crucem lacrymosa
dum pendebat Filius.*

The sorrowful mother stood, weeping near the cross, on which her
son was hanging.

*Cuius animam gementem,
contristatam ac dolentem
pertransivit gladius.*

A sword pierced her sorrowing soul, saddened and suffering.

*O quam tristis et afflicta
fuit illa benedicta
Mater Unigeniti!*

Oh how saddened and afflicted was that blessed one, the Mother of
the Only Begotten!

*Quae moerebat et dolebat
Pia Mater, dum videbat
Nati poenas inclyti.*

The loving mother lamented and grieved when she saw the pain of
her glorious son.

*Quis est homo qui non fleret
Matrem Christi si videret
in tanto supplicio?*

What man is there who would not weep to see the Mother of Christ in such affliction?

> *Quis non posset contristari,*
> *Matrem Christi contemplari*
> *dolentem cum Filio?*

Who could not be moved to contemplate the Mother of Christ grieving with her Son?

This hymn was popular by the second half of the fourteenth century. It has been attributed to Jacopone da Todi (1230–1306). Notable musical settings include those of Josquin des Prés, Palestrina, Scarlatti and Pergolesi.

Dying with Christ
Book of Common Prayer

There should be no greater comfort to Christian persons, than to be made like unto Christ, by suffering patiently adversities, troubles and sicknesses. For he himself went not up to joy, but first he suffered pain; he entered not into his glory before he was crucified. So truly our way to eternal joy is to suffer here with Christ; and our door to enter into eternal life is gladly to die with Christ; that we may rise again from death, and dwell with him in everlasting life.

(From the Visitation of the Sick)

Love so amazing
Isaac Watts

> When I survey the wondrous cross
> On which the Prince of glory died,
> My richest gain I count but loss,
> And pour contempt on all my pride.

Forbid it, Lord, that I should boast,
Save in the death of Christ my God!
All the vain things that charm me most,
I sacrifice them to His blood.

See from His head, His hands, His feet,
Sorrow and love flow mingled down!
Did e'er such love and sorrow meet,
Or thorns compose so rich a crown?

His dying crimson, like a robe,
Spreads o'er His body on the tree;
Then I am dead to all the globe,
And all the globe is dead to me.

Were the whole realm of nature mine,
That were a present far too small;
Love so amazing, so divine,
Demands my soul, my life, my all.

*By Isaac Watts (1674–1748), and published in 1707. It was designed to be
sung at the Eucharist.* Hymns Ancient and Modern *and* The Methodist
Hymn Book *both omit the fourth stanza*

Hide me in thy wounds
Anima Christi

Soul of Christ, sanctify me.
Body of Christ, save me.
Blood of Christ, inebriate me.
Water from the side of Christ, wash me.
Passion of Christ, strengthen me.
O good Jesus, hear me.
Within Thy wounds, hide me.
Separated from Thee let me never be.
From the malignant enemy, defend me.
At the hour of death, call me.

To come to Thee, bid me,
That I may praise Thee in the company
Of Thy Saints, for all eternity. Amen

This prayer, known in Latin as the Anima Christi, *is sometimes thought to be by Ignatius Loyola, because he quotes it in his* Spiritual Exercises. *But it was written by an unknown author some time in the fourteenth century. There had long been a devotion to the wounds of Christ, including the idea, unsympathetic to some modern minds, of hiding within them. The notion is also expressed metaphorically by a Calvinist hymn writer, the Church of England clergyman Augustus Montague Toplady (1740–78) in his 'Rock of Ages'. The identifying of the rock from which Moses derived water in the desert with the spear-wound in Christ's side from which lifegiving water flowed was an idea familiar in medieval readings of the Bible.*

The sign of the cross

In the name of the Father and of the Son and of the Holy Spirit. Amen.

These words, invoking the three persons of the Holy Trinity, are said when a cross is made by touching with the right hand the brow, the breast and the two shoulders in the form of a cross. Orthodox Christians touch the right shoulder first and Catholics the left first, but it is hard to read any real significance into the variation. The sign of the cross is also made on objects or when blessing people and things. It is directed in the Book of Common Prayer to be made during the sacrament of Baptism.

The origins of the sign are not known, but they are most ancient. 'In all our travels and movements,' wrote Tertullian (who was born about the year 160), 'in all our coming in and going out, in putting on of our shoes, at the bath, at the table, in lighting our candles, in lying down, in sitting down, whatever employment occupies us, we mark our foreheads with the sign of the cross.'

In the fourth century St Cyril of Jerusalem writes in his Catecheses: *'Let us then not be ashamed to confess the Crucified. Be the cross our seal, made with boldness by our fingers on our brow and in every thing; over the bread we eat and the cups we drink, in our comings and in goings; before our sleep, when we lie down and when we awake; when we are travelling, and when we are at rest.'*

Before a crucifix

Behold, O good and most sweet Jesus, I fall upon my knees before Thee, and with most fervent desire beg and beseech Thee that Thou wouldst impress upon my heart a lively sense of faith, hope and charity, true repentance for my sins, and a firm resolve to make amends. And with deep affection and grief, I reflect upon Thy five wounds, having before my eyes that which Thy prophet David spoke about Thee, O good Jesus: 'They have pierced my hands and feet, they have counted all my bones.' Amen.

There is a Latin version of this prayer, beginning 'En ego, O bone et dulcissime Iesu . . .'. *Devotion to the five wounds of Christ was popular all over Europe in the fifteenth and sixteenth centuries. Earlier, in the year 1206, St Francis of Assisi had been moved to change his life when, during prayer before a crucifix at San Damiano, outside Assisi, he heard the voice of Jesus telling him to mend the chapel where it hung. The crucifix of San Damiano depicts the mysteries of the Resurrection and the Ascension of Jesus into heaven, and also shows Mary, the Mother of Jesus, and St John the Apostle standing on each side of the cross. Carved figures of Mary and John flanking the crucifix in the chancel arch, above the rood beam, were standard fittings in medieval churches in Britain.*

Christ is risen
The Missal

Dic nobis Maria,
Quid vidisti in via?

Tell us, Mary: say
what thou didst see upon the way.

Sepulcrum Christi viventis,
et gloriam vidi resurgentis:

The tomb the Living did enclose;
I saw Christ's glory as He rose!

Angelicos testes,
sudarium et vestes.

The angels there attesting;
shroud with grave-clothes resting.

Surrexit Christus spes mea:
praecedet suos in Galilaeam.

Christ, my hope, has risen:
He goes before you into Galilee.

This extract is from the Victimae Paschale, *the Sequence (a chant before the Gospel) for Easter Sunday. The author is unknown, though several names have been suggested from the eleventh and twelfth centuries.*

Easter
Book of Common Prayer

Almighty God, who through thy only begotten Son Jesus Christ hast overcome death and opened unto us the gate of everlasting life, we humbly beseech thee that, as by thy special grace preventing us, thou dost put in our minds good desires, so by thy continual help we may bring the same to good effect; through Jesus Christ our Lord, who liveth and reigneth with thee and the Holy Ghost, now and ever. Amen.

Easter dialogue
Joseph Beaumont

First Angel
Those funeral tears why dost thou shed
On life's and resurrection's bed?

Second Angel
Why must those lowering clouds of sadness
Deflower this virgin morn of gladness?

Magdalene
What morn of gladness, now the sun
Of all my fairest joys is gone:
He, whom my soul did hope to meet,
Here in this west in which he set?
But oh! that more than deadly spite
Which robbed him of his life's sweet light
Lives here, you see, in death's own cave,
And plunders Him e'en of His grave;
Nor know I where our foes have set
His body, and my soul with it.

Jesus
Woman, to what loss do thine eyes
Such full drink-offerings sacrifice?

Magdalene
Sweet gardener, if thy hand it were
Which did transplant Him, tell me where
Thou setst that precious root on whom
Grow all my hopes; and I will from
That soil remove Him to a bed
With balm and myrrh and spices spread,
Where by mine eyes' two fountains He
For evermore shall watered be.

Jesus
Mary!

Magdalene
O, Master!

Angels First and Second
With what sweet
Fury she flies at His dear feet,
To weep and kiss out what she by
Her tongue could never signify!
Oh, no! the powers of sweetest tongues,
Of string, or pipe-attended songs,
Can raise no pitch of joy so high

As Easter's rising majesty.
Oh! glorious resurrection, which doth rise
Above the reach of loftiest ecstasies.

Joseph Beaumont (1616–99) was elected Fellow of Peterhouse, Cambridge, in 1636, at the same time as Richard Crashaw. He was accused in 1640 of 'commending Legendary Stories & fabulous tales of the vertue of the Crosse to fellow Commoners & others of the Colledge', and in 1644 he was among the Fellows ejected by parliamentary warrant. After the restoration of the King in 1660, Beaumont's fortunes were reversed and he was elected Master of Peterhouse, in which office he died at the age of 83 of griping of the stomach after delivering the University sermon against Gunpowder Treason.

7

Eucharist

Let us give thanks
The Missal

V: The Lord be with you.
R: And with your spirit.
V: Lift up your hearts.
R: We have raised them up to the Lord.
V: Let us give thanks to the Lord our God.
R: It is meet and right to do so.

Indeed it is meet and right, fitting and profitable that we should always and everywhere give thanks to you, holy Lord, almighty Father, eternal God.

Communion with Jesus is a feature common to all Christian life, in obedience to his command, 'Do this in memory of me.' Holy Communion is also known as the Eucharist, the meaning of which is 'thanksgiving'. Thanksgiving for the gift of Communion itself is involved in the habit of thanksgiving for all that comes from God.

The three couplets of dialogue above (V may be taken for 'Verse'; R for 'Response') are an extraordinarily ancient fragment from the earliest prayers for the Eucharist. They are found in the second-century liturgy of St Hippolytus and in the almost equally old eucharistic prayer of Addai and Mari still used in Iraq. The exchange is still found in the Communion Service of the Book of Common Prayer and in the Roman Missal.

The theme of thanksgiving is then taken up in the ordinary commencement of the Preface of the eucharistic prayer which precedes the praises 'Holy, Holy, Holy'.

In his edition of The Golden Legend *(1483), William Caxton explained the dialogue in these terms:*

And there the priest beginneth the Preface, which is so called, for that it is the preparation or first apparel that goeth before the sacrifice principal, and therefore he saluteth in saying: *Dominus vobis-cum*, in saying that we prepare or make us ready so that our Lord may be and dwell with us, and the people answereth: *Et cum spiritu tuo*. And thus the people and the priest both pray each for other.

After, the priest inciting us saith: *Sursum corda*, that is to say that the people heave their hearts upon high toward God. Then answereth the people: *Habemus ad dominum*, that is to say: 'We heave them to God', and therefore the people, that there in such hour or in that time hath not set their hearts to God may of light lie.

After, the priest saith: *Gratias agamus domino deo nostro*, that is to say: 'Yield we graces and thankings to God.' For if the people in that time hath some devotion, they ought to laud and thank God there-for, and for this, the clerk, for all the people, answereth: *Dignum et justum est*, 'Right even so', as we would say: Worthy and lawful thing is to laud God, just thing is to honour him, and there the priest maketh mention how the angels and archangels and all the court of heaven praise and laud God. And for this at the end he prayeth, that with that foresaid company we all may praise and laud God, saying with firm devotion: *Sanctus, sanctus, sanctus*.

Love's welcome

George Herbert

Love bade me welcome: yet my soul drew back,
    Guiltie of dust and sinne.
But quick'eyd Love, observing me grow slack
    From my first entrance in,
Drew nearer to me, sweetly questioning,
    If I lackd any thing.

A guest, I answerd, worthy to be here:
    Love said, You shall be he.
I the unkinde, ungratefull? Ah my deare,
    I cannot look on thee.
Love took my hand, and smiling did reply,
    Who made the eyes but I?

Truth Lord, but I have marrd them: let my shame
    Go where it doth deserve.
And know you not, sayes Love, who bore the blame?
    My deare, then I will serve.
You must sit down, sayes Love, and taste my meat:
    So I did sit and eat.

George Herbert (1593–1633) set himself the task of following the ideal of the country parson in the Church of England.

Bread of angels
Liturgy of the hours

Panis angelicus, fit panis hominum.
Dat panis caelicus figuris terminum:
O res mirabilis, manducat Dominum
Pauper, servus et humilis.

The bread of angels becomes the bread of men.
The bread of heaven puts an end to types and shadows;
O how wonderful that one who is poor, lowly and humble
    should consume his Lord.

Because of its popularity as an anthem set to music by Cesar Franck and others, this prayer is more familiar in Latin than in English. It forms part of the hymn for matins on the feast of Corpus Christi.

The present Trinity
The Missal

Lord Jesus Christ, Son of the living God, by the will of the Father and the work of the Holy Spirit, your death brought life to the world. By your holy Body and Blood, free me from all my sins and from every evil. Keep me faithful to your teaching and never let me be parted from you.

(From the Communion rite)

Act of confidence
Lady Lucy Herbert

My Lord, notwithstanding my unworthiness, I will go with confidence to receive you, because I am sick and infirm, and you assure me that the Physician is for them and not for the well; and moreover, you being the Lamb of God that takes away the sins of the world, I will go in hopes that you will take away mine.

Lady Lucy Herbert (1669–1744) was a daughter of the Marquess of Powis, but left home aged 24 to join the convent of the Augustinian Canonesses at Bruges. In her day, both in the Catholic Church and the Church of England, reception of Holy Communion was usually a rare event. While aware of the astonishingly elevated nature of the Eucharist, she wrote in terms of confident devotion.

Be heartened
John Keble

Be not disheartened, those specially who have tried in simplicity and obedience to prepare themselves for those Holy Mysteries, and, it may be, are downcast at hearing so much more said than they seem to feel, or understand or enter into.

I say to such, be not disheartened.

The Holy Women by our LORD'S grave knew not at first the full meaning, the full blessing, of their finding it empty; so you, though you try to keep Easter, and to communicate in true faith and repentance, yet cannot go along with the great things you hear set forth of His Resurrection and His Holy Communion.

Well, be of good cheer; it is not your understanding which Jesus requires, so much as your true good will.

Go on humbly doing right, keeping the Commandments, bearing crosses, for the love of your good Saviour; and, in the humble hope of pleasing Him, come with that mind to His Holy Altar.

He will secretly bless you now, and in His good time will teach you all that remains for you to know, that you, with His Saints, may have the fulness of His Blessing.

John Keble (1792–1866), though an instigator of the Oxford Movement, remained a country parson. But he was ready to defend the doctrines of the Real Presence of Jesus in the Eucharist and the teaching of Eucharistic sacrifice, at the trials of Archdeacon Denison in 1853 and of Bishop Forbes of Brechin in 1858. He published his ideas in On Eucharistical Adoration *(1857).*

Jesus' presence
Thomas Aquinas

Adoro te devote, latens Deitas,
Quae sub his figuris vere latitas:
Tibi se cor meum totum subiicit,
Quia te contemplans totum deficit.

Godhead here in hiding, whom I do adore,
Masked by these bare shadows, shape and nothing more,
See, Lord, at thy service low lies here a heart
Lost, all lost in wonder at the God thou art.

Visus, tactus, gustus in te fallitur,
Sed auditu solo tuto creditur.
Credo quidquid dixit Dei Filius:
Nil hoc verbo Veritatis verius.

Seeing, touching, tasting are in thee deceived:
How says trusty hearing? that shall be believed;
What God's Son has told me, take for truth I do;
Truth himself speaks truly or there's nothing true.

In cruce latebat sola Deitas,
At hic latet simul et humanitas;
Ambo tamen credens atque confitens,
Peto quod petivit latro paenitens.

On the cross thy godhead made no sign to men,
Here thy very manhood steals from human ken:
Both are my confession, both are my belief,
And I pray the prayer of the dying thief.

Plagas, sicut Thomas, non intueor;
Deum tamen meum te confiteor.
Fac me tibi semper magis credere,
In te spem habere, te diligere.

I am not like Thomas, wounds I cannot see,
But can plainly call thee Lord and God as he;
Let me to a deeper faith daily nearer move,
Daily make me harder hope and dearer love.

O memoriale mortis Domini!
Panis vivus, vitam praestans homini!
Praesta meae menti de te vivere
Et te illi semper dulce sapere.

O thou our reminder of Christ crucified,
Living Bread, the life of us for whom he died,
Lend this life to me then: feed and feast my mind,
There be thou the sweetness man was meant to find.

Pie pellicane, Iesu Domine,
Me immundum munda tuo sanguine.
Cuius una stilla salvum facere
Totum mundum quit ab omni scelere.

Bring the tender tale true of the Pelican;
Bathe me, Jesu Lord, in what thy bosom ran –
Blood whereof a single drop has power to win
All the world forgiveness of its world of sin.

Iesu, quem velatum nunc aspicio,
Oro fiat illud quod tam sitio;
Ut te revelata cernens facie,
Visu sim beatus tuae gloriae. Amen.

Jesu, whom I look at shrouded here below,
I beseech thee send me what I thirst for so,
Some day to gaze on thee face to face in light
And be blest for ever with thy glory's sight. Amen.

Thomas Aquinas (1225–74) brought Aristotelian philosophy to bear in understanding Christian doctrine, with the aid of a thorough knowledge of Scripture and the early fathers of the Church. His hymn to Jesus present in the Eucharist is still used in worship, and the English translation here was made by Gerard Manley Hopkins (1844–89).

Friend and brother
Richard of Chichester

Thanks be to Thee, my Lord Jesus Christ
For all the benefits Thou hast given me,
For all the pains and insults
Which Thou has borne for me.
O most merciful Redeemer, Friend, and Brother,
May I know Thee more clearly,
Love Thee more dearly,
And follow Thee more nearly,
Day by day. Amen.

This prayer is attributed to St Richard of Chichester, otherwise known as Richard of Wyche. As a reforming bishop of Chichester he had a hard time with Henry III. He died in 1253 and was declared a saint in 1262. Pilgrims flocked to seek his intercession and pray at his tomb in Chichester Cathedral.

Unity
Richard Challoner

A prayer when the priest spreads his hands over the oblation.

We present to thee, O Lord, this bread and wine, which being composed of many, reduced into one, are symbols of concord and unity, that by thy all-powerful blessing they may be made for us the precious body and blood of thy beloved Son; and that through him, and through his death and Passion, applied to our souls by these sacred mysteries, we may obtain mercy, grace, and peace in this life, and eternal happiness in the next.

This prayer takes up the idea of an ancient prayer in an anonymous book called the Didache: *'As this broken bread was scattered upon the mountains and being gathered together became one, so may thy Church be gathered together from the ends of the earth into Thy kingdom.' Here it is proposed as a devotional aid for worshippers during the solemn and silent moment of offering in the Canon of the Mass in the Tridentine rite. It appeared in* The Garden of the Soul, *the best known prayerbook compiled by Richard Challoner (1691–1781). Though it was an enduringly popular work among the minority Catholics in the eighteenth century and beyond, the full text of the 1741 edition was republished by the Church of England's Society of Saints Peter and Paul in 1916.*

Jesus Christ the Apple Tree
Christina Rossetti

As the Apple Tree among the trees of the wood,
So is my Beloved among the sons. (Song of Solomon 2:3)

O Lord Jesus Christ, Who art as the Apple Tree among the trees of the wood, give us to taste of Thy Sweetness; that eating we may yet be hungry, and drinking we may yet be thirsty.

Infuse of Thy Sweetness, I pray Thee, into Thy servants, that cleaving to Thee they may attract others also to Thee: until as the hart desireth the water brooks, all souls may long after Thee, O God. Amen.

Christina Rossetti (1830–94), in this extract from Annus Domini *(1874), follows tradition in interpreting the words of the Song of Solomon figuratively with reference to Jesus Christ. The reference to the hart desiring the water brooks is to Psalm 42.*

Countless gifts
Catherine Winkworth

Now thank we all our God,
With heart and hands and voices,
Who wondrous things has done,
In Whom this world rejoices;
Who from our mothers' arms
Has blessed us on our way
With countless gifts of love,
And still is ours today.

O may this bounteous God
Through all our life be near us,
With ever joyful hearts
And blessed peace to cheer us;
And keep us in His grace,
And guide us when perplexed;
And free us from all ills,
In this world and the next!

All praise and thanks to God
The Father now be given;
The Son and him Who reigns
With them in highest heaven;
The one eternal God,
Whom earth and heaven adore;
For thus it was, is now,
And shall be evermore.

Catherine Winkworth (1827–78), who popularized the German choral tradition in England, included her translation of 'Nun danket' in her collection Lyra Germanica, *published in 1858. The hymn was written by Martin Rinkart (1586–1649), a Lutheran minister, who worked with fortitude and charity during famine and pestilence during the Thirty Years' War. It is based on some verses in the first chapter of Ecclesiasticus. The hymn is included in both* Hymns Ancient and Modern *and* The Methodist Hymn Book. *The usual tune derives from one published for the hymn in 1647, but Mendelssohn introduced some adjustments.*

8

Reconciliation

With a great cry
Anon, AD 1000

O Lord, hear my prayer, for I know already that my time is near at hand. Grant to me, O Lord, wisdom and understanding, and enlighten my heart that I may know Thee always all the days of my life, for Thou art God, and there is none other but Thou alone; who hast come down from heaven, and by Thy Holy Spirit hast filled Mary with light.

Thee, therefore, O my God, do I humbly entreat that Thou wilt enlighten my heart, for my sins are without number exceedingly. Grant me, O Lord, I beseech Thee, that I may be able to bewail them through faith and charity and through Thy wondrous Name.

I adjure Thee that in whatever day I call upon Thee, Thou wilt deign to hear me speedily as Thou didst graciously hear the prayer of Tobias and of Sara.

Pour out to me tears of the heart, as Thou didst lay the foundations of the earth upon the waters, for my heart has grown hard as if a stone; I have sinned, O Lord, I have sinned exceedingly in my life; I acknowledge all my iniquities. I entreat of Thee; to Thee do I cry.

Do Thou stretch out Thy right hand and deliver me from my adversary as Thou didst deliver the Three Children from the furnace of burning fire. Therefore I pray Thee, O God, heavenly King, give me temperance and chastity, humbleness and faithfulness and truth, that I may be found worthy to persevere in good works. As indeed the desire of my heart is, whatever it be I have said or thought or done from my youth upwards.

I beseech Thee, O Lord; to Thee do I cry with a great cry out of my whole heart. I praise thee, I magnify Thee, with all Thy holy apostles and martyrs. Do Thou deign to send to my help Thine angels and apostles [manuscript damaged] I pray thee, holy Mary, Mother of my Lord, and all the holy Virgins, that they will hear me and

intercede with Thee for me a sinner, and obtain for me to come into
the way of truth.

*This prayer, composed in southern England 1,000 years ago, was twice
almost destroyed by fire. The surviving scorched vellum manuscript, which
belongs to the British Museum, was examined by the remarkable self-taught
liturgiologist Edmund Bishop (1846–1917) on a train journey from Devon
to London in 1906. The translation above is his, and the author of the
prayer, he noted, 'spoke simply out of his whole heart, and his words strike
straight home'.*

*The hundred years before the Norman Conquest, Bishop noted, was, like
the end of the seventh century, a period of 'extraordinary outflow of devotional products, especially of prayers, characteristic of their own particular
epoch'.*

*Another ancient manuscript of the same prayer attributes it to St Gregory,
though there is no evidence that it was of his composition.*

Intolerable burden
Book of Common Prayer

Almighty God,
Father of our Lord Jesus Christ,
Maker of all things, judge of all men;
We acknowledge and bewail our manifold sins and wickedness,
Which we, from time to time, most grievously have committed,
By thought, word, and deed,
Against thy Divine Majesty,
Provoking most justly thy wrath and indignation against us.
We do earnestly repent,
And are heartily sorry for these our misdoings;
The remembrance of them is grievous unto us;
The burden of them is intolerable.
Have mercy upon us,
Have mercy upon us, most merciful Father;
For thy Son our Lord Jesus Christ's sake,
Forgive us all that is past;
And grant that we may ever hereafter Serve and please thee

In newness of life,
To the honour and glory of thy Name;
Through Jesus Christ our Lord. Amen.

(Confession, from the service for Holy Communion)

Rend my rocky heart
Thomas Traherne

O Thou Sun of Righteousness,
Ecclypsed on the Cross,
overcast with Sorrows,
and covered with the shadow of Death,
remove the vail of thy flesh that I may see thy Glory.
Those cheeks are shades,
those Limbs and Members clouds,
that hide the Glory of thy Mind,
thy Knowledge and thy Love from us.
But were they removed
those inward Excellencies would remain Invisible.
As therefore we see thy Flesh with our fleshly Eyes,
and handle thy Wounds with our Bodily Sences,
let us see thy Understanding with our Understandings,
and read thy Love with our own.
Let our Souls have Communion with thy Soul,
and let the Eye of our Mind enter into thine.
Who art Thou who Bleeding here
causest the Ground to Tremble and the Rocks to rend,
and the Graves to Open?
Hath thy Death Influence so high as the highest Heavens?
That the Sun also Mourneth and is Clothed in Sables?
Is thy Spirit present in the Temple,
that the vail rendeth in twain at thy Passion?
O let me leave Kings' Courts to come unto Thee,
and chuse rather in a Cave to serve Thee,
than on a Throne to despise Thee.
O my Dying Gracious Lord,

I perceive the virtue of thy Passion every where:
Let it I beseech Thee enter into my Soul,
and rend my Rocky Stony Heart,
and tear the vail of my flesh
that I may see into the Holy of Holies!
O Darken the Sun of Pride and Vain Glory.
Yea let the Sun it self be Dark
in Comparison of thy Love!
And open the Grave of my flesh,
that my Soul may arise to Praise Thee.
Grant this for thy Mercy sake. Amen!

This is the eighty-eighth in the First Century of Meditations *by Thomas Traherne (1637–74). He is contemplating the passage from the Gospel (Matthew 27:45) that says 'Now from the sixth hour there was darkness over all the land unto the ninth hour . . . And, behold, the veil of the temple was rent in twain from the top to the bottom; and the earth did quake, and the rocks rent; and the graves were opened; and many bodies of the saints which slept arose.'*

Act of contrition
Traditional

O my God, I am sorry and beg pardon for all my sins, and detest them above all things, because they deserve thy dreadful punishments, because they have crucified my loving Saviour Jesus Christ and, most of all, because they offend thy infinite goodness; and I firmly resolve, by the help of thy grace, never to offend thee again, and carefully to avoid the occasions of sin. Amen.

New hearts
Book of Common Prayer

Almighty and everlasting God, who hatest nothing that thou hast made and dost forgive the sins of all them that are penitent, create and make in us new and contrite hearts, that we, worthily lamenting our sins and acknowledging our wretchedness, may obtain of thee, the God of all mercy, perfect remission and forgiveness; through Jesus Christ. Amen.

(Collect for Ash Wednesday)

Three fatal sisters
Robert Herrick

Three fatall Sisters wait upon each sin;
First, Fear and Shame without, then Guilt within.

From His Noble Numbers or His Pious Pieces *(1647) by Robert Herrick (1591–1674), a priest of the Church of England and a poet whose art seemed easy.*

Becoming whole
George MacDonald

Thy beasts are sinless, and do live before thee;
Thy child is sinful, and must run to thee.
Thy angels sin not and in peace adore thee;
But I must will, or never more be free.
I from thy heart came, how can I ignore thee?
Back to my home I hurry, haste, and flee;
There I shall dwell, love-praising evermore thee.

My holy self, thy pure ideal, lies
Calm in thy bosom, which it cannot leave;
My self unholy, no ideal, hies
Hither and thither, gathering store to grieve.
Not now, O Father! now it mounts, it flies,
To join the true self in thy heart that waits,
And, one with it, be one with all the heavenly mates.

Trusting thee, Christ, I kneel, and clasp thy knee;
Cast myself down, and kiss thy brother-feet.

One self thou and the Father's thought of thee!
Ideal son, thou hast left the perfect home,
Ideal brother, to seek thy brothers come!
Thou know'st our angels all, God's children sweet,
And of each two wilt make one holy child complete.

George MacDonald (1824–1905) in The Diary of an Old Soul *(in which this extract forms the entries for 19–21 December) presents the idea of God's ideal for us and our unhealed, unholy selves as two entities that need to be reunited.*

Deliver us
Book of Common Prayer

From all evil and mischief; from sin; from the crafts and assaults of the devil; from thy wrath, and from everlasting damnation,
    Good Lord, deliver us.

From all blindness of heart; from pride, vainglory, and hypocrisy; from envy, hatred, and malice, and all uncharitableness,
    Good Lord, deliver us.

From fornication, and all other deadly sin; and from all the deceits of the world, the flesh, and the devil,
    Good Lord, deliver us.

(From the Litany)

Jesus lost
Richard Challoner

1. Consider how Jesus, Mary, and Joseph went every year up to Jerusalem, to the Temple of God, upon the solemn festivals, notwithstanding their poverty and their living at the distance of three days' journey from Jerusalem. There they employed the weeks appointed for the feast in assisting at the public worship, praises, and sacrifices which, at those times, were offered to God in the temple. Christians, learn from this example the diligence with which you ought to assist

at the public worship of God upon festivals. Learn not to suffer every trifling difficulty to hinder your attendance in God's temple on those days, when neither the length nor the difficulties either of the journey, or of the stay they were to make in Jerusalem, could keep this holy family from the constant observance of these times dedicated to God. But who can conceive the dispositions of soul with which they entered upon these journeys; their recollection on the road, their heavenly conversation in Jerusalem, their profound adoration, their inflamed love, their fervent prayer and devotion in the temple! Let us strive to imitate them.

2. Consider how when Jesus was twelve years old, and they had gone up, according to their custom, to keep the solemn Feast of the Pasch in Jerusalem, after the days of the solemnity were fulfilled – when they returned, our Saviour withdrew Himself from them and stayed behind in the city. They, innocently thinking Him to be in the company, went one day's journey homewards without Him, and then not finding Him, were struck with unspeakable grief and concern for their loss: the more so because they apprehended, lest by some fault of theirs, they had driven Him away from them. What anguish must it be to a soul, that is sensible of the treasure she possesses when Jesus is with her, to find that He has withdrawn Himself from her, that she has lost her treasure. But how much more must this blessed couple have regretted the loss of Jesus: their love for Him being much greater than can be expressed or imagined! For in proportion to their love, their sorrow must have been great beyond expression. Learn hence, my soul, that value thou oughtest to set upon the happiness of having Jesus with thee; and how much thou oughtest to regret the loss of Him.

3. Consider that although the Blessed Virgin and St Joseph had lost Jesus as to His sensible presence, yet they had not lost Him as to the presence of His grace and love; they had Him still very near to them, because they had Him in their hearts. A lesson for Christians of goodwill, not to be discouraged, nor to give themselves up to excessive anguish, if sometimes they experience the like subtraction of the sensible presence of our Lord, by dryness in their devotions, and spiritual desolation; let them but take care to keep their heart and will with Him, and they may be assured He is not far from them. He has often dealt thus with the greatest saints – and to their advantage

too – to keep them humble and distrustful of themselves; and to teach them not to seek their own satisfaction in the milk of spiritual consolations, but to be content to feed their souls with the more solid diet of conformity to the will of God and the cross of Christ.

Conclusion. Take care not to drive away Jesus by wilful sin; and be assured that nothing else can ever separate Him from thee.

On seeking Jesus, when He has been lost by sin.

1. Consider how great an evil it is to lose Jesus by wilful sin. It is far greater loss than if we should lose our all. This loss is the greatest misery that can befall a soul on this side of eternity – it wants nothing but eternity to make it hell. And yet how common is this loss? How often is Jesus lost in this manner, even in our most solemn festivals, by the abuse of these holy times! And how is it possible that a Christian should feel any comfort, joy or pleasure under so great a loss? What then must they do, who have reason to apprehend they have thus lost their Jesus: that He is now no longer theirs, and they no longer His! They must learn from the Blessed Virgin and St Joseph how they are to seek and find Him again; for though this blessed couple had not lost Him in that wretched way, yet the manner in which they sought Him may be instructive to others, to teach them by what means Jesus may be found again when He is lost.

2. Consider that the Blessed Virgin and St. Joseph were no sooner aware they had lost Jesus, but they began to seek Him without delay, and gave themselves no rest till they had found Him: to teach us that there ought to be no delay in seeking Him as soon as we perceive we have lost him, and how much we ought to regret so sad a loss. They made no stay in the place where they were, but hastened back to Jerusalem, to seek Him; not enduring to remain for ever so short a time at a distance from Him: to teach us to spare no pains, either night or day, in seeking Him, and in using all means in our power to find Him. They sought Him sorrowing, that is, with their souls full of grief and anguish, through the sense they had of the loss of their beloved: to teach us that the true way of finding Jesus when lost must be by sorrow joined with love, that is, by a contrite and humble heart. They sought Him with perseverance, and did not give over their search till they had found Him: to teach us not to desist, on meeting with difficulties and opposition, in our search after Jesus, but to go on with diligence till we recover His gracious company.

3. Consider that Jesus was not found by the Blessed Virgin and St Joseph amongst their kindred and acquaintance. Alas he is too often lost in the company and conversation of our worldly friends: and is seldom to be found there. The common conversation of the world is at best empty, worldly, and distracting: and it is out of fashion to speak or think of Jesus in the company of worldlings. Therefore the soul that would effectually find Him, must withdraw as much as may be from worldly company and enter into a kind of spiritual retreat; she must make the best of her way by spiritual reading, meditation, and prayer, to the temple of God in Jerusalem; or rather she must make a temple for Jesus within her own self, and seek Him there by recollection. This is the surest place to find Him. Sinners, return to your own hearts, and you will quickly find your God. When you went astray from Him, you went astray also from your own hearts and your inward house; you forgot at the same time both God and yourselves. Return home to your interior, and you shall recover both again.

Conclusion. If at any time you have reason to apprehend that you have lost Jesus, withdraw immediately from the crowd to seek Him in His temple in your own interior, and give yourselves no rest till you have found Him there. There He will hear you, and will teach you.

This consideration on the Gospel of the Sunday within the Octave of the Epiphany appeared in Meditations for Every Day of the Year *by Richard Challoner (1691–1781). He had been received into the Catholic Church as a teenager by John Gother, chaplain at Warkworth Manor, Northamptonshire, where the young Challoner's mother was a servant. After education at Douai, Challoner began his work of explaining Christian teaching in plain prose with a book called* Think well on't, or, Reflections on the great truths of the Christian religion for every day in the month *(1728). The most famous of his 60 or so books is* The Garden of the Soul *(1740), but he was also responsible for revising the Rheims-Douai Bible in more current language. From 1740 he served as a bishop, with authority in the extensive London District. He lived a simple life and was known for his practical charity.*

In peril on the sea
Book of Common Prayer

Most powerful and glorious Lord God, at whose command the winds blow, and lift up the waves of the sea, and who stillest the rage thereof. We thy creatures, but miserable sinners, do in this our great distress cry unto thee for help: Save, Lord, or else we perish. We confess, when we have been safe, and seen all things quiet about us, we have forgot thee our God, and refused to hearken to the still voice of thy word, and to obey thy commandments: But now we see, how terrible thou art in all thy works of wonder; the great God to be feared above all: And therefore we adore thy Divine Majesty, acknowledging thy power, and imploring thy goodness. Help, Lord, and save us for thy mercy's sake in Jesus Christ thy Son, our Lord. Amen.

(From the Prayers to be used in Storms at Sea)

None should perish
Christina Rossetti

The Lord is not slack concerning His Promise, as some men count slackness; but is longsuffering to us-ward, not willing that any should perish, but that all should come to repentance. (2 Peter 3:9)

O Lord Jesus Christ, Who art not slack concerning Thy Promise, but longsuffering to us-ward, I plead with Thee for every human soul: O Lord help us, bring us to repentance, give us grace and peace, grant us glory and joy in the day of Thy promised coming.

Help those who know Thee not, to know and love Thee; those who know Thee, to love Thee and live after Thy Pattern. Help us all, I entreat Thee, up the steep hill of salvation into the heavenly garden of Thy planting. Amen.

Christina Rossetti (1830–94) in this extract from Annus Domini *(1874) echoes her famous couplet expressing the uphill nature of Christian struggle, 'Does the road wind uphill all the way? / Yes, to the very end.' But she knows that on the heavenly mountain a garden is planted.*

God's promises
Book of Common Prayer

God, who declarest thy almighty power most chiefly in showing mercy and pity, give unto us abundantly thy grace, that we, running to thy promises, may be made partakers of thy heavenly treasure; through Jesus Christ our Lord. Amen.

(Collect for the Eleventh Sunday after Trinity)

No outcast
John Keble

Do not think that you are in the way to be an outcast, though the sense of your imperfection lie ever so grievous upon you. But still, while you humble yourself, be bold and steadfast in loving and serving God, and in trying to do all your duty. In this way you will turn the vexing and mortifying thought, the gnawing sense of your own imperfection, into an exercise of true contrition: it will do your soul much good.

Bodily suffering
Book of Common Prayer

God, who knowest us to be set in the midst of so many and great dangers, that for man's frailness we cannot always stand uprightly, grant to us the health of body and soul that all those things which we suffer for sin, by thy help we may well pass and overcome; through Christ our Lord. Amen.

(Collect for the Fourth Sunday after Epiphany)

Coolness and balm

J. G. Whittier

Dear Lord and Father of mankind,
Forgive our foolish ways;
Reclothe us in our rightful mind,
In purer lives Thy service find,
In deeper reverence, praise.

In simple trust like theirs who heard,
Beside the Syrian sea,
The gracious calling of the Lord,
Let us, like them, without a word,
Rise up and follow Thee.

O Sabbath rest by Galilee,
O calm of hills above,
Where Jesus knelt to share with Thee
The silence of eternity,
Interpreted by love!

With that deep hush subduing all
Our words and works that drown
The tender whisper of Thy call,
As noiseless let Thy blessing fall
As fell Thy manna down.

Drop Thy still dews of quietness,
Till all our strivings cease;
Take from our souls the strain and stress,
And let our ordered lives confess
The beauty of Thy peace.

Breathe through the heats of our desire
Thy coolness and Thy balm;
Let sense be dumb, let flesh retire;
Speak through the earthquake, wind, and fire,
O still, small voice of calm.

By John Greenleaf Whittier (1807–92), known as America's 'Quaker Poet'. It formed the concluding part of his seventeen-stanza poem called 'The Brewing of Soma'. Soma, a name later appropriated by Aldous Huxley for the feelgood drug in Brave New World, *was known in the nineteenth century to have been the drink supposed to have induced religious stupor among the forebears of speakers of Indo-European languages.*

The poem was prefaced by a quotation from the Sanskrit poem 'Vashista' translated by Max Muller, the Oxford philologist, who rather admired the ancient religion of India: 'These libations mixed with milk have been prepared for Indra: offer Soma to the drinker of Soma.'

Whittier, by contrast, not only disapproved of the ancient priests' soma-toping, but of a wide variety of more or less dionysian practices: 'The scourger's keen delight of pain, the Dervish dance, the Orphic strain, the wild-haired Bacchant's yell, the desert's hair-grown hermit; the naked Santon, haschish-drunk, the cloister madness of the monk, the fakir's torture show!'

The hymn is included in both Hymns Ancient and Modern *and* The Methodist Hymn Book. *As a hymn, or prayer, the six stanzas above work much better detached from the stanzas that originally preceded them. Many people read it with their minds on the tune by Sir Hubert Parry (written for his own oratorio* Judith*).*

As we forgive those . . .
Book of Common Prayer

Grant us, O Lord, to learn to love our enemies, by the example of thy martyr Saint Stephen, who prayed to thee for his persecutors; who liveth and reigneth with thee and the Holy Ghost, now and ever. Amen.

(Collect for St Stephen's Day)

For enemies
Anselm

Forbid it, O good Lord, forbid it that I should be to my brethren an occasion of death, that I should be to them a stone of stumbling and rock of offence.

For it is enough and more than enough that I should be an offence unto myself; mine own sin is sufficient for me.

96

Thy servant entreateth Thee for his fellow-servants that they should not on my account offend so great and good a Master, but be reconciled to Thee, and agree with me according to Thy will for Thy sake.

This is the vengeance which my inmost heart desireth to ask of Thee upon my fellow-servants, mine enemies and fellow-sinners.

This is the punishment which my soul asketh upon my fellow-servants and enemies, that they should love Thee and one another, according to Thy will and as is expedient for us, so that we may satisfy our common Master both as concerning ourselves and as concerning one another and serve our common Lord in unity by the teaching of charity and common good.

This vengeance I, Thy sinful servant, pray may be prepared against all those that wish me evil and do me evil.

Do Thou prepare this also, most merciful Lord, against Thy sinful servant likewise.

Anselm (1033–1109), even before he became Archbishop of Canterbury, knew from his own experience what it was to have enemies who wished him ill. Instead of heaping coals on their heads, he asks for the only kind of vengeance that leaves the avenger as happy as his enemies.

In my bosom a sun
Henry Vaughan

How rich, O Lord, how fresh Thy visits are!
'Twas but just now my bleak leaves hopeless hung,
   Sullied with dust and mud;
Each snarling blast shot through me, and did share
Their youth and beauty; cold showers nipt, and wrung
   Their spiciness and blood;
But since Thou didst in one sweet glance survey
Their sad decays, I flourish, and once more
   Breathe all perfumes and spice;
I smell a dew like myrrh, and all the day
Wear in my bosom a full sun; such store
   Hath one beam from Thy eyes.

Henry Vaughan (1621–95) in this poem from Silex Scintillans, *the collection he compiled in the 1650s, uses the imagery of nature to express the reviving of the soul under grace after a dark night.*

9

The Holy Spirit

The Comforter
Book of Common Prayer

God, who as upon this day hast taught the hearts of thy faithful people by the sending to them the light of thy Holy Spirit, grant us by the same Spirit to have a right judgement in all things and evermore to rejoice in his holy comfort; through the merits of Christ Jesus our Saviour, who liveth and reigneth with thee, in the unity of the same Spirit, one God, world without end. Amen.

Collect for Whitsunday. Cranmer's English is a translation of the ancient Latin collect for the Mass of Pentecost or Whitsunday:

Deus, qui (hodierna die) corda fidelium Sancti Spiritus illustratione docuisti: da nobis in eodem Spiritu recta sapere, et de eius semper consolatione gaudere. Per Christum Dominum nostrum.

That collect has also been turned into a prayer for private devotion, with the omission of the words 'hodierna die' and the addition beforehand of two parts of the Alleluia before the Gospel of Pentecost. In Latin this goes:

Veni Sancte Spiritus, reple tuorum corda fidelium.
Et tui amoris in eis ignem accende.
Emitte spiritum tuum et creabuntur.
Et renovabis faciem terare.

Come, Holy Spirit, fill the hearts of your faithful.
And kindle in them the fire of your love.
Send forth your Spirit and they shall be created.
And you will renew the face of the earth.

Dwell in me

Anselm

Now, O Thou Love that art the bond of the Godhead,
Thou that art the holy Love which is betwixt the Father Almighty
    and His most blessed Son,
Thou Almighty Spirit,
the Comforter, the most merciful consoler of them that mourn,
do Thou enter by Thy mighty power
into the innermost sanctuary of my heart,
and of Thy goodness dwell therein,
making glad with the brightness of Thy glorious light the neglected
    corners thereof, and making fruitful by the visitation of Thine
    abundant dew the fields that are parched and barren with long
    continued drought.
Pierce with the arrows of Thy love the secret chambers of the inner
    man.
Let the entrance of Thy healthful flames set the sluggish heart
    alight, and the burning fire of Thy sacred inspiration enlighten
    it and consume all that is within me, both of mind and body.
Give me drink of Thy pleasures as out of the river;
so that I may take no pleasure hereafter in the poisonous sweetness
    of worldly delights.
Give sentence with me, O God, and defend my cause against the
    ungodly people.
Teach me to do the thing that pleaseth Thee, for Thou art my God.
I believe that in whomsoever Thou dost dwell, Thou makest there
    an habitation for the Father and for the Son.
Blessed is he who shall be counted worthy to entertain Thee;
because by Thee the Father and the Son shall make their abode
    with him.

*Anselm (1033–1109) spent 33 years as a monk at the abbey of Bec before his
election as Archbishop of Canterbury. In these years of study and prayer he
repeatedly returned to the mystery of the Holy Trinity, attempting to understand with reason what he believed with faith.*

Light of life

John Austin

Come, Holy Ghost, send down those beams,
Which sweetly flow in silent streams
From Thy bright throne above.

O come, Thou Father of the poor;
O come, Thou source of all our store,
Come, fill our hearts with love.

O Thou, of comforters the best,
O Thou, the soul's delightful guest,
The pilgrim's sweet relief.

Rest art Thou in our toil, most sweet
Refreshment in the noonday heat;
And solace in our grief.

O blessed Light of life Thou art;
Fill with Thy light the inmost heart
Of those who hope in Thee.

Without Thy Godhead nothing can,
Have any price or worth in man,
Nothing can harmless be.

Lord, wash our sinful stains away,
Refresh from heaven our barren clay,
Our wounds and bruises heal.

To Thy sweet yoke our stiff necks bow,
Warm with Thy fire our hearts of snow,
Our wandering feet recall.

Grant to Thy faithful, dearest Lord,
Whose only hope is Thy sure word,
The sevenfold gifts of grace.

Grant us in life Thy grace that we,
In peace may die and ever be,
In joy before Thy face.

Amen. Alleluia.

John Austin (1613–69), a Lincolnshire man who became a Catholic at Cambridge, included this version of the venerable Sequence for Pentecost, Veni sancta spiritus, et emitte caelitus *(by Stephen Langton, 1150–1228, Archbishop of Canterbury) in his* Devotions in the Ancient Way of Offices *(1668). This book was far more influential than the lack of fame of its title suggests. It was adapted for Anglican use by Theophilus Dorrington in 1686, and again in 1700 by Susanna Hopton. It formed the basis for Nathaniel Spinckes's* The True Church of England – Man's Companion in the Closet *(1721), adapted once more in the nineteenth century by Francis Paget for a market enlivened by the Oxford Movement. Beyond his work as a translator, Austin was also an innovator in composing 40 original hymns for private use in his* Devotions, *some of them included by John Wesley in his* Collection of Psalms and Hymns.

Sent by the Trinity
William Caxton

The Blessed Holy Feast of Pentecost or of the Holy Ghost.

The Holy Ghost, as witnesseth St Luke in the story of the Acts of the Apostles, on this day was sent to the apostles in the form and likeness of tongues of fire.

He was sent from the Father, and from the Son he was sent, and he also himself, the Holy Ghost, gave and sent himself.

Of the first saith St John (Chapter 14) 'The Holy Ghost, which is said *paraclitus*, whom God the Father shall send in my name, this is he that shall teach us all.'

Of the second saith St John (16:7): 'If I go, saith Jesus, I shall send him to you.'

Now it is, to wit, that the sending is compared in three manners to the sender:

First, as he that giveth being in his substance, and in this manner the sun giveth his rays or beams.

Secondly, as in giving virtue or strength, and so is the dart given by the virtue and strength of him that casteth it.

Thirdly, to him that giveth his jurisdiction to another, and thus the messenger is sent from him of whom he hath the commandment.

And after these three manners the Holy Ghost may be said to be sent, for it is said: sent of the Father and of the Son as having virtue and authority in his operation, notwithstanding himself giveth and sendeth him. The which thing seemed to be veritable after this that the gospel of John saith, (16:13): *Cum autem venerit ille Spiritus veritatis,* etc., 'When the spirit of truth shall come, which proceedeth from the Father, he shall bear witness of me that he cometh from me.'

Now, saith St Leo in a sermon of the Pentecost, 'The incommutable deity of the Blessed Trinity is without any changing, one in substance, not divided in operation, all one in will, like in omnipotence, equal in glory, and in his mercy. He hath taken to himself the work of our redemption, that the Father be to us merciful, the Son to us profitable, and God the Holy Ghost inflame us. And because that the Holy Ghost is God, therefore he giveth himself.'

And that this is true, St Ambrose in the book of the Holy Ghost sayeth thus: 'The glory of the Divinity is approved by four reasons: for that he is without sin, for that he leaveth [takes away] the sins, for that he is creator and not creature, for that he worshipped none but he is worshipped.'

And in that is showed to us that the Blessed Trinity was all given to us, for the Father hath offered all that he had. As saith St Austin [Augustine of Hippo]: 'He hath sent to us his Son in price of our redemption, and the Holy Ghost in sign of our adoption.'

Semblably [in like manner] the Son of God hath given himself unto us. For thus saith St Bernard: 'He is our pastor, he is our pasture, and he is our redemption, for he gave his soul in price of our redemption, his blood in to drink, his flesh in to meat, and his divinity in to final reward.'

Semblably the Holy Ghost gave himself all to us; like as the apostle saith: 'By the Holy Ghost is given the word of sapience to one, to another of science; and thus of all graces particular is given by the same Holy Ghost' (1 Corinthians 12:8).

These notes on Pentecost come in The Golden Legend, *originally by Jacobus de Voragine, translated and edited by William Caxton and printed in 1483.*

Steadfast repose

George Hickes

O God, leave me not a moment to my own human frailty without
the assistance of Thy Holy Spirit;
But let Him constantly inspire me with fear, love, and devotion
towards Thee;
with truth, justice, and charity towards my neighbour;
and with abstinence and sobriety towards myself.
And because I live in evil times,
and am in danger of being deceived by the wiles and false
pretensions of men,
let Him be also unto me a Spirit of wisdom and conduct, and
discretion;
that in all my conversation I may be able to discern truth from
hypocrisy;
and sincere, understanding, and faithful friends, from false,
designing flatterers.
Furthermore, I beseech Thee, let Him be unto me a Spirit of
patience under
all crosses, and in all provocations;
a Spirit of trust, and steadfast repose of mind, in Thy care and
providence;
a Spirit of forgiveness to my enemies;
a Spirit of humility to make me quiet and easy in myself,
meek and gentle to others,
and to free me from all the sin and torment of pride, envy, and
ambition:
and finally, so let him guide and govern me,
through the whole course of my short life here,
that I may not fail to attain everlasting life,
through Jesus Christ our Lord.
Amen.

*This extract from a long prayer to God the Father on Whitsunday was com-
posed by George Hickes (1642–1715) and appeared in Nathaniel Spinckes's*
True Church of England Man's Companion in the Closet *(1721),
which became known as Spinckes's* Devotions *during its long usage in the
eighteenth century.*

10

Communion of saints

In God's eye, Christ
Gerard Manley Hopkins

As kingfishers catch fire, dragonflies draw flame;
As tumbled over rim in roundy wells
Stones ring; like each tucked string tells, each hung bell's
Bow swung finds tongue to fling out broad its name;
Each mortal thing does one thing and the same:
Deals out that being indoors each one dwells;
Selves goes itself; *myself* it speaks and spells,
Crying, *What I do is me: for that I came.*

I say more: the just man justices;
Keeps grace: that keeps all his goings graces;
Acts in God's eye what in God's eye he is –
Christ – for Christ plays in ten thousand places,
Lovely in limbs, and lovely in eyes not his
To the Father through the features of men's faces.

*Gerard Manley Hopkins (1845–89) had an intuition of the individual activ-
ity of each being. Each has, as it were, a vocation to be itself. The phrase 'for
that I came' echoes the words of Jesus to Pilate: 'To this end was I born, and
for this cause came I into the world, that I should bear witness unto the truth'
(John 18:37). The just man, with God's grace, acts in unity with Christ, and,
as part of his mystical body, is Christ.*

One body

John Donne

Now, this Bell tolling softly for another, saies to me, Thou must die.

Perchance hee for whom this Bell tolls, may be so ill, as that hee knowes not it tolls for him; And perchance I may thinke my selfe so much better than I am, as that they who are about mee, and see my state, may have caused it to toll for mee, and I know not that.

The Church is Catholike, universall, so are all her Actions. All that she does, belongs to all. When she baptizes a child, that action concernes mee; for that child is thereby connected to that Head which is my Head too, and engrafted into that body whereof I am a member. And when she buries a Man, that action concernes me. All mankinde is of one Author, and is one volume; when one Man dies, one Chapter is not torne out of the booke, but translated into a better language; and every Chapter must be so translated. God emploies several translators; some peeces are translated by age, some by sicknesse, some by warre, some by justice; but God's hand is in every translation; and his hand shall binde up all our scattered leaves againe, for that Librarie where every booke shall lie open to one another.

As therefore, the Bell that rings to a Sermon, calls not upon the Preacher onely, but upon the Congregation to come; so this Bell calls us all: but how much more mee, who am brought so neere the doore by this sicknesse. There was a contention as farre as a suite, (in which both pietie and dignitie, religion, and estimation, were mingled) which of the religious Orders should ring to praiers first in the Morning; and it was determined, that they should ring first that rose earliest. If we understand aright the dignitie of this Bell that tolls for our evening prayer, wee would bee glad to make it ours, by rising early, in that application, that it might bee ours, as wel as his, whose indeed it is.

The Bell doth toll for him that thinkes it doth; and though it intermit againe, yet from that minute, that that occasion wrought upon him, hee is united to God. Who casts not up his Eie to the Sunne when it rises? Who bends not his eare to any bell, which upon any occasion rings? But who can remove it from that bell, which is passing a peece of himselfe out of this world?

105

No man is an Iland, intire of it selfe; every man is a peece of the Continent, a part of the maine; if a Clod bee washed away by the Sea, Europe is the lesse, as well as if a Promontorie were, as well as if a Mannor of thy friend's or of thine owne were; any man's death diminishes me, because I am involved in Mankinde. And therefore never send to know for whom the bell tolls; It tolls for thee.

Neither can we call this a begging of Miserie or a borrowing of Miserie, as though we were not miserable enough of our selves, but must fetch in more from the next house, in taking upon us the Miserie of our Neighbours. Truly it were an excusable covetousnesse if wee did; for affliction is a treasure, and scarce any man hath enough of it. No man hath affliction enough that is not matured, and ripened by it, and made fit for God by that affliction. If a man carry treasure in bullion, or in a wedge of gold, and have none coined into currant Monies, his treasure will not defray him as he travels. Tribulation is Treasure in the nature of it, but it is not currant money in the use of it, except wee get nearer and nearer our home, Heaven, by it.

Another man may be sicke too, and sick to death, and this affliction may lie in his bowels, as gold in a Mine, and be of no use to him; but this bell, that tells me of his affliction, digs out, and applies that gold to me, if by this consideration of another's danger, I take mine owne into contemplation, and so secure my selfe, by making my recourse to my God, who is our onely securitie.

Expostulation

My God, my God, is this one of thy waies, of drawing light out of darknesse, to make him for whom this bell tolls, now in this dimnesse of his sight, to become a superintendent, an overseer, a Bishop, to as many as heare his voice, in this bell, and to give us a confirmation in this action? Is this one of thy waies to raise strength out of weaknesse, to make him who cannot rise from his bed, nor stirre in his bed, come home to me, and in this sound, give mee the strength of healthy and vigorous instructions?

O my God, my God, what Thunder is not a well-tuned Cymball, what hoarsenesse, what harshnesse is not a cleare Organ, if thou bee pleased to set thy voice to it? And what Organ is not well plaied on, if thy hand bee upon it? Thy voice, thy hand is in this sound, and in this one sound, I heare this whole consort.

I heare thy Jacob call unto his sonnes, and say; Gather your selves together, that I may tell you what shall befall you in the last daies. He saies, That which I am now, you must bee then. I heare thy Moses telling mee, and all within the compasse of this sound, This is the blessing wherewith I blesse you before my death. This, that before your death, you would consider your owne in mine. I heare thy Prophet saying to Ezechias, Set thy house in order, for thou shalt die, and not live. Hee makes us of his familie, and calls this a setting of his house in order, to compose us to the meditation of death. I heare thy Apostle saying, I thinke it meet to put you in remembrance, knowing that shortly I must goe out of this Tabernacle. This is the publishing of his will, and this Bell is our legacie, the applying of his present condition to our use.

I heare that which makes al sounds musique, and all musique perfit; I heare thy Sonne himselfe saying, Let not your hearts be troubled. Only I heare this change, that whereas thy Sonne saies there, I goe to prepare a place for you, this man in this sound saies, I send to prepare you for a place, for a grave.

But, O my God, my God, since heaven is glory and joy, why doe not glorious and joyfull things lead us, induce us to heaven? Thy legacies in thy first will, in the old Testament, were plenty and victorie; Wine and Oile, Milke and Honie, alliances of friends, ruine of enemies, peacefull hearts and cheerfull countenances, and by these galleries thou broughtest them into thy bed-chamber, by these glories and joies, to the joies and glories of heaven. Why hast thou changed thine old way, and carried us by the waies of discipline and mortification, by the waies of mourning and lamentation, by the waies of miserable ends, and miserable anticipations of those miseries, in the appropriating the exemplar miseries of others to our selves, and usurping upon their miseries, as our owne, to our owne prejudice?

Is the glory of heaven no perfecter in it selfe, but that it needs a foile of depression and ingloriousnesse in this world, to set it off? Is the joy of heaven no perfecter in it selfe, but that it needs the sourenesse of this life to give it a taste? Is that joy and that glory but a comparative glory and a comparative joy? Not such in it selfe, but such in comparison of the joilessnesse and the ingloriousnesse of this world? I know, my God, it is farre, farre otherwise.

As thou thy selfe, who art all, art made of no substances, so the joyes and glory which are with thee, are made of none of these circumstances; Essentiall joy, and glory Essentiall. But why then, my God, wilt thou not beginne them here? Pardon, O God, this unthankfull rashnesse; I that aske why thou doest not, finde even now in my selfe, that thou doest; such joy, such glory, as that I conclude upon my selfe, upon all, They that finde not joy in their sorrowes, glory in their dejections in this world, are in a fearefull danger of missing both in the next.

Prayer

Eternall and most gracious God, who has beene pleased to speake to us, not onely in the voice of Nature, who speakes in our hearts, and of thy word, which speakes to our eares, but in the speech of speechlesse Creatures, in Balaams Asse, in the speech of unbelieving men, in the confession of Pilate, in the speech of the Devill himselfe, in the recognition and attestation of thy Sonne, I humbly accept thy voice in the sound of this sad and funeral bell.

And first, I blesse thy glorious name, that in this sound and voice I can heare thy instructions, in another man's to consider mine owne condition; and to know, that this Bell which tolls for another, before it come to ring out, may take in me too. As death is the wages of sinne, it is due to mee; as death is the end of sicknesse, it belongs to mee. And though so disobedient a servant as I, may be afraid to die, yet to so mercifull a Master as thou, I cannot be afraid to come.

And therefore, into thy hands, O my God, I commend my spirit, a surrender, which I know thou wilt accept, whether I live or die; for thy servant David made it, when he put himselfe into thy protection for his life; and thy blessed Sonne made it, when hee delivered up his soule at his death. Declare thou thy will upon mee, O Lord, for life or death, in thy time. Receive my surrender of my selfe, now. Into thy hands, O Lord, I commend my spirit.

And being thus, O my God, prepared by thy correction, mellowed by thy chastisement, and conformed to thy will, by thy Spirit, having received thy pardon for my Soule, and asking no reprieve for my Body, I am bold, O Lord, to bend my prayers to thee, for his assistance, the voice of whose bell hath called mee to this devotion. Lay hold upon his soule, O God, till that soule have thoroughly considered his account, and how few minutes soever it have to remaine in that body, let the power of thy Spirit recompence the shortnesse of time, and perfect his account, before he passe away. Present his sinnes so to him, as that he may know what thou forgivest, and not doubt of thy forgiveness; let him stop upon the infiniteness of those sinnes, but dwell upon the infiniteness of thy Mercy. Let him dis-

cerne his owne demerits, but wrap himselfe up in the merits of thy
Sonne, Christ Jesus. Breath inward comforts to his heart, and afford
him the power of giving such outward testimonies thereof, as all that
are about him may derive comforts from thence, and have this edifi-
cation, even in this dissolution, that though the body be going the
way of all flesh, yet that soule is going the way of all Saints.

When thy Sonne cried out upon the Crosse, My God, My God,
Why hast thou forsaken me? He spake not so much in his owne
Person, as in the person of the Church, and of his afflected
members, who in deep distresses might feare thy forsaking. This
patient, O most blessed God, is one of them; in his behalfe, and in
his name, heare thy Sonne crying to thee, My God, my God, why hast
thou forsaken me? And forsake him not; but with thy left hand lay
his body in the grave, (if that bee thy determination upon him) and
with thy right hand receive his soule into thy Kingdome, and unite
him and us in one Communion of Saints. Amen

*The famous passage, 'Never send to know for whom the bell tolls . . .' is seldom
seen in context, more seldom yet read with the subsequent passages headed
'Expostulation' and 'Prayer'. The* Devotions upon Emergent Occasions
(1624) *by John Donne (1572–1631) is made up of 23 sets of meditations,
expostulations and prayers following the course of a sickness that brought the
poet near death. Though death is here the focus, it is caught up in considerations of the mystical Body of Christ, the Communion of Saints.*

Gifts in each member
John Keble

Let this be the lesson settled in our hearts at this great and holy time;
to believe that we are Christian brethren indeed, and to cherish in
our hearts true brotherly feeling one towards another. The Coming
of God the Holy Ghost from Heaven, to dwell in our hearts and
bodies, and unite us to Jesus Christ, is so great, so vast an event, that
it may well overwhelm and confound our minds, if we try to think of
it all at once, and to feel all we might and ought from it: it is well that
we should select some one point of what it teaches, and meditate on

it with all our hearts: and let this one subject to-day be, the One Holy Spirit, with His differing gifts, abiding alike in every member of Christ.

John Keble (1792–1866) had sold huge numbers of his collection of religious poems, The Christian Year, *and had made a name as one of the instigators of the Oxford Movement. But from 1836 he settled as a country parson at Hursley, Hampshire, where he remained for the 30 years until his death. His sermons filled ten posthumous volumes.*

A nesting place
Christina Rossetti

'Rooms shalt thou make in the ark' (Genesis 6.14): but the literal Hebrew (see margin of Authorised Version) says not 'rooms' but 'nests'.

Now without for one moment calling in question that these particular 'nests' were rooms, the special word employed does yet suggest a special train of thought.

The Ark: the Church. Destruction without, safety within. 'A dispensation of the Gospel' is vouchsafed to man, and woe is us if we accept not the offered salvation.

We do (please God) accept it. However unworthily, we occupy rooms in the spiritual Ark: there we live, and there we hope to die.

The rooms being commodiously and thoroughly furnished unto good works, the tenants are thereby invited to perform such good works as belong to their several vocations.

So to do becomes our duty. And it is constituted no less our privilege, seeing that to crown all it has promise of a reward.

Christian duties, Christian privileges: some honest Christians do much, and upbraid themselves for not doing more. They labour and are heavy laden, they are careful and cumbered; making a task of duty, and task of privilege, a task of life, and a most formidable task of death.

The vastness and still more the loftiness of their 'room' overwhelms them: 'Who is sufficient for these things?' is their prevalent forlorn feeling. At times they would almost be ready (if they dared) to say: 'It were better to dwell in a corner of the housetop.'

They comport themselves as if too little for their own greatness. They appear like savage man consumed and dwindling away in the face of a civilisation too high for him.

But wherefore contemplate their allotted room as a lofty and vast palace of well-nigh uninhabitable grandeur: as this, and as nothing more?

Our room, as God builds and makes it for us, is likewise our nest: and a nest is surely the very homeliest idea of a home.

From Time Flies: A Reading Diary *(1885) by Christina Rossetti (1830–94).*

Lighting us
Henry Vaughan

God's saints are shining lights: who stays
    Here long must pass
O'er dark hills, swift streams, and steep ways
    As smooth as glass;
    But these all night,
    Like candles, shed
    Their beams, and light
    Us into bed.

They are – indeed – our pillar fires,
    Seen as we go;
They are that City's shining spires
    We travel to:
    A swordlike gleam
    Kept man for sin
    First *out;* this beam
    Will guide him *in.*

These lines are from the poem 'Joy of my life' in the book Silex Scintillans, *by Henry Vaughan (1621–95). The 'swordlike gleam' is the fiery sword of the angel posted at the gate of paradise when Adam and Eve were expelled.*

All generations
Book of Common Prayer

My soul doth magnify the Lord: and my spirit hath rejoiced in God
   my saviour.

For he hath regarded the lowliness of his handmaiden.

For behold, from henceforth all generations shall call me blessed.

For he that is mighty hath magnified me and holy is his Name.

And his mercy is on them that fear him throughout all generations.

He hath showed strength with his arm: he hath scattered the proud
   in the imagination of their hearts.

He hath put down the mighty from their seat: and hath exalted the
   humble and meek.

He hath filled the hungry with good things: and the rich he hath
   sent empty away.

He remembering his mercy hath holpen his servant Israel: as he
   promised to our forefathers, Abraham and his seed, for ever.

Glory be to the Father, *&c.*

As it was in the beginning, *&c.*

Magnificat anima mea Dominum;
Et exultavit spiritus meus in Deo salutari meo,
Quia respexit humilitatem ancillae suae; ecce enim ex hoc beatam me dicent
   omnes generationes.
Quia fecit mihi magna qui potens est, et sanctum nomen eius,
Et misericordia eius a progenie in progenies timentibus eum.
Fecit potentiam in brachio suo;
Dispersit superbos mente cordis sui.
Deposuit potentes de sede, et exaltavit humiles.
Esurientes implevit bonis, et divites dimisit inanes.
Suscepit Israel, puerum suum, recordatus misericordiae suae,
Sicut locutus est ad patres nostros, Abraham et semini eius in saecula.

*This canticle is taken directly from the first chapter of Luke's Gospel. In Latin
it is used every day at Vespers in the Liturgy of the Hours, and this usage was
retained in the English liturgy of Evensong after the Reformation. The
English of the Prayer Book of 1662 is very close to that of 1549, including the
archaic 'holpen'. Its Latin version is very familiar to those who hear it in
worship or through recordings of its many musical settings.*

The Magnificat anchors the Virgin Mary, the mother of Jesus, firmly in the Communion of Christians throughout time. They are one body insofar as they are members of Christ, who as man is Mary's son and as God is son of the eternal Father.

Sub tuum praesidium
Traditional

We fly to thy patronage, O holy Mother of God; despise not our petitions in our necessities, but deliver us always from all dangers, O glorious and blessed Virgin. Amen.

Sub tuum praesidium confugimus, Sancta Dei Genetrix. Nostras deprecationes ne despicias in necessitatibus nostris, sed a periculis cunctis libera nos semper, Virgo gloriosa et benedicta. Amen.

This is the earliest known prayer asking for the intercession of the Virgin Mary. It has been found in an Egyptian papyrus from the third century.

Fertile tears
Aldhelm

Most excellent lady and holy virgin mother, mercifully hear the prayers of the people who water their parched faces with tears and strike the earth with bended knee, for they merit pardon by the outpouring of a fountain of tears and they blot out the sins of their lives by their continual prayers.

> *Femina praepollens et sacra puerpera virgo,*
> *Audi clementer populorum vota precantum,*
> *Marcida qui riguis umectant imbribus ora*
> *Ac genibus tundunt curvato poplite terram,*
> *Dum veniam fuso lacrimarum fonte merentur*
> *Et crebris precibus delent peccamina vitae.*

Aldhelm, Abbot of Malmesbury, died in 710. This piece of verse was written as an inscription for a church dedicated to St Mary the Virgin.

An angel's message
Book of Common Prayer

We beseech thee, Lord, pour thy grace into our hearts, that, as we have known Christ thy Son's incarnation by the message of an angel, so by his cross and passion we may be brought unto the glory of his resurrection; through the same Christ our Lord. Amen.

This collect for the Annunciation of the Virgin Mary is Thomas Cranmer's translation of the prayer that accompanied the antiphon Alma Redemptoris Mater, *said at compline during the Advent weeks leading up to Christmas.*

Our Lord and Our Lady
Hilaire Belloc

They warned Our Lady for the Child
That was Our Blessed Lord,
And She took Him into the desert wild,
Over the camel's ford.

And a long song She sang to Him
And a short story told:
And she wrapped Him in a woollen cloak
To keep Him from the cold.

But when Our Lord was grown a man
The Rich they dragged Him down,
And they crucified Him in Golgotha,
Out and beyond the Town.

They crucified Him on Calvary,
Upon an April day;
And because He had been Her little Son
She followed Him all the way.

Our Lady stood beside the Cross,
A little space apart,
And when She heard Our Lord cry out
A sword went through her heart.

They laid Our Lord in a marble tomb,
Dead, in a winding sheet.
But Our Lady stands above the world
With the white Moon at her feet.

Hilaire Belloc (1870–1953) wrote a great number of books, some undistin-guished and some bombastic. He is much enjoyed for his humorous verse Cautionary Tales *and admired for his travel book* The Path to Rome *(1902), but he could write poetry of lasting value too.*

Star of the sea
Alcuin

Virgin Mary, mother of God, virgin most chaste, light and star of the sea, queen of our salvation.

> *Virgo Maria dei genitrix, castissima virgo,*
> *Lux et stella maris, nostrae regina salutis.*

Alcuin (735–804), a man of learning and a poetic genius, had a lasting influence on the public worship of the Church. Much material in the Book of Common Prayer, as well as the Roman Missal, can be traced to him. He also composed tituli or inscriptions for churches and altars, intended to prompt devotion in those who read them.

Salve

Hermann Contractus

Hail, holy Queen, Mother of mercy;
hail, our life, our sweetness and our hope.
To thee do we cry, poor banished children of Eve.
To thee do we send up our sighs,
mourning and weeping in this vale of tears.
Turn then, most gracious advocate,
thine eyes of mercy towards us;
and after this our exile, show unto us the blessed fruit of thy
    womb, Jesus.
O clement, O loving, O sweet Virgin Mary!

*This anthem is used in the Liturgy of the Hours from Trinity Sunday until
the Saturday before Advent. Its authorship has been attributed to Hermann
Contractus (1014–54), whose surname indicated his crippled body. But he
acquired a reputation as a fine mathematician and poet. He is also thought to
have written the plainsong music to accompany the anthem. The popularity of
the Salve endured in the Renaissance. Columbus's men sang it on Saturday
evenings on deck as they sailed to unknown lands. Thomas More consoled his
family, on the prospect of his losing his state office, with the thought that they
could go from door to door singing the Salve and asking for alms.*

All seafarers

John Paul II

O Mary, Star of the Sea, light of every ocean,
guide seafarers across all dark and stormy seas that they
    may reach the haven of peace and light prepared in Him
    who calmed the sea.
As we set forth upon the oceans of the world and cross the
    deserts of our time,
show us, O Mary, the fruit of your womb,
for without your Son we are lost.
Pray that we will never fail on life's journey,

that in heart and mind, in word and deed,
in days of turmoil and in days of calm,
we will always look to Christ and say,
'Who is this that even wind and sea obey him?'
Our Lady of Peace, pray for us!
Bright Star of the Sea, guide us!

John Paul II (1920–2005) was elected Pope in 1978, when he was 58. He saw devotion to the Virgin Mary as a way of coming closer to Jesus Christ, who as God and man is the one who has brought about the reconciliation of fallen mankind. Just as the Salve was a prayer popular with seafarers, so this prayer has been adopted in Britain by the Apostleship of the Sea, which ministers to sailors.

Remember
Traditional

Remember, O most sweet and loving Virgin Mary, that it is a thing unheard of that anyone ever had recourse to your protection, implored your help, or sought your intercession, and was left forsaken. Filled, therefore, with confidence in your goodness, I fly to you, O Mother, Virgin of virgins! To you I come, before you I stand, a sorrowful sinner. Despise not my words, O Mother of the Word, but graciously hear and grant my prayer. Amen.

Attributed to St Bernard of Clairvaux (1090–1153), but probably wrongly, the prayer, usually known by its Latin name, the Memorare, was popularized by Claude Bernard (1588–1641).

11

Angels

Heaven and earth
Book of Common Prayer

Everlasting God, who hast ordained and constituted the services of all angels and men in a wonderful order, mercifully grant that they who always do thee service in heaven may by thy appointment succour and defend us in earth; through Jesus Christ our Lord, who liveth and reigneth with thee and the Holy Ghost now and ever. Amen.

Collect for Saint Michael and All Angels. Cranmer's English renders the Latin of the collect for the Mass of St Michael.

They walk with us
Augustine Baker

An exercise to the angels

1. I salute you, O holy spirits,
    and with all my heart congratulate your happiness,
    who continually contemplate the Divine Face and all-satiating Goodness;
2. You, O Seraphim, Cherubim, and Thrones, who are of the higher hierarchy;
    you, O Dominations, Virtues, and Powers, of the middle;
    you, O Princes, Archangels, and Angels, of the lowest,
    who continually sing, Holy, Holy, Holy, Lord God of Sabaoth.
3. Thou, O my Lord, hast made these holy spirits angels for my benefit,
    and hast commanded them to keep me in all Thy ways.

4. They do therefore assist us with great care,
   and with watchful endeavour at all times and in all places
   succouring us.
5. They present our sighs and sobs to Thee, O Lord;
   they inflame our wills,
   illuminate our understandings,
   and replenish our minds with holy thoughts.
6. They walk with us in all our ways,
   rejoicing at our virtues
   and contristated at our vices.
7. Their love is great and excessive towards us.
8. They help such as are taking pains;
   they protect such as are at rest;
   they encourage such as fight;
   they crown the conquerors;
   they rejoice with such as joy (I mean such as joy in Thee);
   and they suffer with such as suffer (I mean such as are in
   sufferance for Thee).
9. Great and very great is the honour done to man
   to have angels to wait on and assist him.
10. O my dear Angel Guardian,
    govern, protect, and defend me;
    illuminate, comfort, and direct me, now and evermore.
11. O blessed angels,
    be you ever blessed and praised for all and every favour and
    benefit you have most lovingly and powerfully bestowed on me
    and vouchsafed me.
12. Grant, O Father of heaven and earth,
    that they may ever rejoice concerning us (that is, by our
    practice of virtue),
    and that Thou mayest ever be praised by them and us;
    and that both they and we may be brought into one sheepfold,
    that together we may confess to Thy holy name,
    O Thou Creator of men and angels. Amen.

Augustine Baker (1575–1641) was a lawyer in London who became a Benedictine monk. The spiritual advice that he compiled when a chaplain to English nuns at Cambrai was edited after his death by Serenus Cressy and published as Sancta Sophia *in 1657. It became a spiritual classic.*

Guardian angel
Anonymous

Angel of God,
my guardian dear,
To whom God's love commits me here;
Ever this day [night] be at my side,
To light, to guard, to rule and guide.

A Latin version of this prayer may have been written in England in the twelfth century.

My oldest friend
John Henry Newman

My oldest friend, mine from the hour
    When first I drew my breath;
My faithful friend, that shall be mine,
    Unfailing, till my death;

Thou hast been ever at my side;
    My Maker to thy trust
Consign'd my soul, what time He framed
    The infant child of dust.

No beating heart in holy prayer,
    No faith, inform'd aright,
Gave me to Joseph's tutelage,
    Or Michael's conquering might.

Nor patron Saint, nor Mary's love,
    The dearest and the best,
Has known my being, as thou hast known,
    And blest, as thou hast blest.

Thou wast my sponsor at the font;
     And thou, each budding year,
Didst whisper elements of truth
     Into my childish ear.

And when, ere boyhood yet was gone,
     My rebel spirit fell,
Ah! thou didst see, and shudder too,
     Yet bear each deed of Hell.

And then in turn, when judgements came,
     And scared me back again,
Thy quick soft breath was near to soothe
     And hallow every pain.

And thou wilt hang about my bed,
     When life is ebbing low;
Of doubt, impatience, and of gloom,
     The jealous sleepless foe.

Mine, when I stand before the Judge;
     And mine, if spared to stay
Within the golden furnace, till
     My sin is burn'd away.

And mine, O Brother of my soul,
     When my release shall come;
Thy gentle arms shall lift me then,
     Thy wings shall waft me home.

'I used to wish the Arabian Tales were true', wrote John Henry Newman (1801–90) in 1823, looking back to his childhood. 'I thought life might be a dream, or I an Angel, and all this world a deception, my fellow-angels by a playful device concealing themselves from me, and deceiving me with the semblance of a material world.' But this poem on his guardian angel was not written until he was 52, and living at the Oratorian community he had founded in Birmingham.

Fellow-servants

Christopher Smart

St Michael and All Angels
Angelic natures, great in arms
Against the dragon and his pow'rs,
Whom Michael's excellence alarms
From highest heav'n's imperial tow'rs;
Ye that in Christ his church attend
What time the services are sung,
And your propitious spirits blend
With our united heart and tongue.
O come, celestial watch and ward,
As in the closet I adore,
My fellow-servants of the Lord,
To whom these measures I restore.
If Satan's malice was withstood
Where Moses cold and breathless lay,
Give Michael, patient, meek, and good,
Through Christ, the glory of the day.
If Tobit's charitable soul,
A type of Jesus Christ to come,
Was blessed from the poor man's dole
Ev'n to the social sparrow's crumb;
If to the living and the dead
His hand was rich in deeds of love,
First Raphael from his Master fled
By mandate in the heights above.
If Zacharias was inform'd
That God his pious pray'rs should crown,
The barren womb to ripeness warm'd,
'Twas Gabriel brought the tidings down.
Hail mighty princes in the height,
Which o'er stupendous works preside
Of vast authority and weight –
But there are other pow'rs beside.
These, one for every man, are sent
God in the spirit to reveal,
To forward ev'ry good event,
And each internal grief to heal.

St Michael

Leo XIII

Holy Michael, Archangel,
defend us in the day of battle.
Be our safeguard against the wickedness
and snares of the devil.
May God rebuke him,
we humbly pray;
and do you,
O Prince of the heavenly host,
by the power of God
thrust down to hell Satan
and all the wicked spirits
who wander through the world
for the ruin of souls. Amen.

According to the book of Revelation, St Michael and his angels fought with the dragon of evil. His feast day, 29 September (Michaelmas), is a quarter day in England, a reflection of the former importance accorded him. Drawing on older material, this prayer was drawn up by Pope Leo XIII and directed to be said after Mass.

PART THREE

This Life with God

12

The presence of God

God be in my head
Anonymous

God be in my head, and in my understanding;
God be in mine eyes, and in my looking;
God be in my mouth, and in my speaking;
God be in my heart, and in my thinking;
God be at mine end, and at my departing.

This prayer is widely known with the much-loved musical setting by Sir Walford Davies (1869–1941). The words are usually attributed to a Sarum Primer, or prayer book, of 1538. Primers containing prayers according to the liturgy of Sarum or Salisbury were produced with frequency at home and abroad in the sixteenth century. Many copies perished because they were so well used.

Dwelling in hearts
Anonymous

Glorious and powerful God, we understand
Thy dwelling is on high,
Above the starry sky.
Thou dwell'st not in stone temples made with hands,
But in the flesh hearts of the sons of men.
To dwell is Thy delight
Near hand though out of sight.

We give of Thine own hand, Thy acceptation
Is very life and blood
To all actions good

Whenever here or hence our supplication
From pure and with unfeigned hearts to Thee ascend,
Be present with Thy grace,
Show us Thy loving face.

O down on us full showers of mercy send;
Let Thy love's burning beams
Dry up all our sins' streams.
Arise, O Lord, and come into Thy rest.
Both now and evermore Thy Name be blest;
Founder and foundation
Of endless habitation.

The author of this poem is unknown, but it was published in 1813 in a collection entitled Tixall Poetry, *for the anthology was made from 1634 onwards by Herbert Aston (1614–88) of Tixall, Staffordshire. Some of the poems are by his sisters Gertrude Thimelby and Constance Fowler. Other poems by Constance Fowler remain in manuscript.*

In me and outside
Augustine of Hippo

And how shall I call upon my God, my God and Lord, since, when
I call for Him, I shall be calling Him to myself?
And what room is there within me, whither my God can come into
  me?
Whither can God come into me, God who made heaven and earth?
Is there, indeed, O Lord my God, aught in me that can contain
  Thee?
Do then heaven and earth, which Thou hast made, and wherein
  Thou hast made me, contain Thee?
Or, because nothing which exists could exist without Thee, doth
  therefore whatever exists contain Thee?
Since, then, I too exist, why do I seek that Thou shouldst enter into
  me, who were not, wert Thou not in me?
Why? Because I am not gone down in hell, and yet Thou art there
  also.

For if I go down into hell, Thou art there.
I could not be then, O my God, could not be at all, wert Thou not
    in me;
or, rather, unless I were in Thee,
of whom are all things,
by whom are all things,
in whom are all things?
Even so, Lord, even so.
Whither do I call Thee, since I am in Thee?
Or whence canst Thou enter into me?
For whither can I go beyond heaven and earth, that thence my
    God should come into me, who hath said, I fill the heaven and
    the earth.

Here is St Augustine of Hippo (354–430) in the second chapter of his auto-biographical Confessions, *wondering out loud how God can be in him, since there is no way of containing God. Yet he knows that God is in heaven and earth, which he made (and he refers to the beginning of the Bible, 'In the beginning God created the heaven and the earth', Genesis 1:1). Even in the underworld he would find God, as the Psalmist says, 'If I ascend up into heaven, thou art there: if I make my bed in hell, behold, thou art there' (Psalm 139:8). And in a way all things are in God, as St Paul says, 'For of him, and through him, and to him, are all things: to whom be glory for ever. Amen' (Romans 11:36). The translation is E. B. Pusey's, but it is a little changed version of that by William Watts in 1631. It is easy to get the drift of Augustine, but not the glory of his accomplished Latin rhetoric.*

Christ's hand

R. H. Benson

After a retreat

    What hast thou learnt to-day?
    Hast thou sounded awful mysteries,
    Hast pierced the veiled skies,
    Climbed to the feet of God,
    Trodden where saints have trod,
    Fathomed the heights above?
      Nay,
    This only have I learnt, that God is love.

What hast thou heard to-day?
Hast heard the Angel-trumpets cry,
And rippling harps reply;
Heard from the Throne of flame
Whence God incarnate came
Some thund'rous message roll?
   Nay,
This have I heard, His voice within my soul.

What hast thou felt to-day?
The pinions of the Angel guide
That standeth at thy side
In rapturous ardours beat,
Glowing, from head to feet,
In ecstasy divine?
   Nay,
This only have I felt, Christ's hand in mine.

Robert Hugh Benson (1871–1914) was one of the remarkable children of Edward White Benson, who became Archbishop of Canterbury when Robert was eleven. He wrote a clutch of novels, several historical, but some focusing on the unusual, such as The Lord of the World *(1907), on the Antichrist.*

A new colour
Ronald Knox

You know how, if you are in a very bad temper, with some permanent grievance at the back of your mind, every little worry that happens to you during the day – when the window won't shut properly, when the fire won't burn, when your pipe won't draw, when you drop a stitch, when the soup is cold – every little worry like that jars upon your jangled nerves, and becomes the occasion for a fresh outburst of irritation; the grasshopper has become a burden, the whole day is coloured for you by the original frame of mind in which you started it. Just so, if you are living continually with God, every affection, every desire, every thought, takes its colour from that holy relationship, and, under its influence, takes to itself the wings of prayer.

This observation comes from Bread or Stone, *a set of meditations on prayer, by Ronald Knox (1888–1957).*

Living like a candle
John Bunyan

Man's like a candle in a candlestick,
Made up of tallow and a little wick;
And as the candle is when 'tis not lighted,
So is he who is in his sins benighted.
Nor can a man his soul with grace inspire,
More than can candles set themselves on fire.
Candles receive their light from what they are not;
Men grace from Him for whom at first they care not.
We manage candles when they take the fire;
God men, when he with grace doth them inspire.
And biggest candles give the better light,
As grace on biggest sinners shines most bright.
The candle shines to make another see,
A saint unto his neighbour light should be.
The blinking candle we do much despise,
Saints dim of light are high in no man's eyes.
Again, though it may seem to some a riddle,
We use to light our candles at the middle.
True light doth at the candle's end appear,
And grace the heart first reaches by the ear.
But 'tis the wick the fire doth kindle on,
As 'tis the heart that grace first works upon.
Thus both do fasten upon what's the main,
And so their life and vigour do maintain.
The tallow makes the wick yield to the fire,
And sinful flesh doth make the soul desire
That grace may kindle on it, in it burn;
So evil makes the soul from evil turn.
But candles in the wind are apt to flare,
And Christians, in a tempest, to despair.
The flame also with smoke attended is,
And in our holy lives there's much amiss.
Sometimes a thief will candle-light annoy,
And lusts do seek our graces to destroy.
What brackish is will make a candle sputter;
'Twixt sin and grace there's oft a heavy clutter.

Sometimes the light burns dim, 'cause of the snuff,
Sometimes it is blown quite out with a puff;
But watchfulness preventeth both these evils,
Keeps candles light, and grace in spite of devils.
Nor let not snuffs nor puffs make us to doubt,
Our candles may be lighted, though puffed out.
The candle in the night doth all excel,
Nor sun, nor moon, nor stars, then shine so well.
So is the Christian in our hemisphere,
Whose light shows others how their course to steer.
When candles are put out, all's in confusion;
Where Christians are not, devils make intrusion.
Then happy are they who such candles have,
All others dwell in darkness and the grave.
But candles that do blink within the socket,
And saints, whose eyes are always in their pocket,
Are much alike; such candles make us fumble,
And at such saints good men and bad do stumble.
Good candles don't offend, except sore eyes,
Nor hurt, unless it be the silly flies.
Thus none like burning candles in the night,
Nor ought to holy living for delight.
But let us draw towards the candle's end:
The fire, you see, doth wick and tallow spend,
As grace man's life until his glass is run,
And so the candle and the man is done.
The man now lays him down upon his bed,
The wick yields up its fire, and so is dead.
The candle now extinct is, but the man
By grace mounts up to glory, there to stand.

These verses come from A Book for Boys and Girls *(1686) by John Bunyan (1628–88). It was published with little woodcuts and bears an altogether lighter tone than many of Bunyan's works on sins and grace. The couplet 'Thus none like burning candles in the night,/Nor ought to holy living for delight', has caused some readers to stumble, but it simply means, I think, that there's nothing like candles in the night, and nothing to compare with holy living to produce delight.*

Divine friendship
Thomas Traherne

O the Nobility of Divine Friendship!
Are not all his Treasures yours, and yours His?
Is not your very Soul and Body His;
Is not His Life and Felicity yours?
Is not His Desire yours?
Is not His Will yours?
And if His will be yours,
the Accomplishment of it is yours,
and the end of all is your Perfection.
You are infinitely Rich as He is: Being Pleased in evry thing
as He is.
And if His Will be yours, yours is His – for you will what He
Willeth,
which is to be truly Wise and Good and Holy.
And when you Delight in the same reasons that moved Him
to Will, you will Know it.

This is number 53 in the First Century of Meditations *by Thomas Traherne (1637–74)*.

Knowing Jesus
John Henry Newman

1. The Familiarity of Jesus
I. The Holy Baptist was separated from the world. He was a Nazarite. He went out from the world, and placed himself over against it, and spoke to it from his vantage ground, and called it to repentance. Then went out all Jerusalem to him into the desert, and he confronted it face to face. But in his teaching he spoke of One who should come to them and speak to them in a far different way. He should not separate Himself from them, He should not display Himself as some higher being, but as their brother, as of their flesh and of their bones, as one among many brethren, as one of the multitude and amidst them; nay, He was among them already. 'There is in the midst of you One whom you know not.'

That greater one called Himself the Son of man. He was content to be taken as ordinary in all respects, though He was the Highest. St John and the other Evangelists, though so different in the character of their accounts of Him, agree most strikingly here. The Baptist says, 'There is in the midst of you One whom you know not.'

Next we read of his pointing Jesus out privately, not to crowds, but to one or two of his own religious followers; then of their seeking Jesus and being allowed to follow Him home. At length Jesus begins to disclose Himself and to manifest His glory in miracles;

But where? At a marriage feast, where there was often excess, as the architriclinus [steward] implies.

And how? In adding to the wine, the instrument of such excess, when it occurred.

He was at that marriage feast not as a teacher, but as a guest, and (so to speak) in a social way, for He was with His Mother. Now compare this with what He says in St Matthew's Gospel of Himself: 'John came neither eating nor drinking. The Son of man came eating and drinking, and they say: Behold a man that is a glutton and wine-drinker.' John might be hated, but he was respected; Jesus was despised. See also Mark 1:22, 27, 37; 3:21, for the astonishment and rudeness of all about Him. The objection occurs at once. What a marked feature it must have been of our Lord's character and mission, since two Evangelists, so independent in their narrations, record it!

II. This was, O dear Lord, because Thou so lovest this human nature which Thou hast created. Thou didst not love us merely as Thy creatures, the work of Thy hands, but as men. Thou lovest all, for Thou hast created all; but Thou lovest man more than all.

How is it, Lord, that this should be? What is there in man, above others? 'What is man, that Thou art mindful of him?' Who can sound the depth of Thy counsels and decrees? Thou hast loved man more than Thou hast loved the Angels: and therefore, as Thou didst not take on Thee an angelic nature when Thou didst manifest Thyself for our salvation, so too Thou wouldst not come in any shape or capacity or office which was above the course of ordinary human life – not as a Nazarene, not as a Levitical priest, not as a monk, not as a hermit, but in the fulness and exactness of that human nature which so much Thou lovest. Thou camest not only a perfect man, but as proper man; not formed anew out of earth, not with the spiritual body which Thou now hast, but in that very flesh which had fallen in Adam, and with all our infirmities, all our feelings and sympathies, sin excepted.

III. O Jesu, it became Thee, the great God, thus abundantly and largely to do Thy work, for which the Father sent Thee. Thou didst not do it by halves – and, while that magnificence of Sacrifice is Thy glory as God, it is our consolation and aid as sinners. O dearest Lord, Thou art more fully man than the holy Baptist, than St John, Apostle and Evangelist, than Thy own sweet Mother. As in Divine knowledge of me Thou art beyond them all, so also in experience and personal knowledge of my nature.

Thou art my elder brother. How can I fear, how should I not repose my whole heart on one so gentle, so tender, so familiar, so unpretending, so modest, so natural, so humble? Thou art now, though in heaven, just the same as Thou wast on earth: the mighty God, yet the little child – the all-holy, yet the all-sensitive, all-human.

2. Jesus the Hidden God

Be not faithless, but believing

I. I adore Thee, O my God, who art so awful, because Thou art hidden and unseen! I adore Thee, and I desire to live by faith in what I do not see; and considering what I am, a disinherited outcast, I think it has indeed gone well with me that I am allowed, O my unseen Lord and Saviour, to worship Thee anyhow.

O my God, I know that it is sin that has separated between Thee and me. I know it is sin that has brought on me the penalty of ignorance. Adam, before he fell, was visited by Angels. Thy Saints, too, who keep close to Thee, see visions, and in many ways are brought into sensible perception of Thy presence. But to a sinner such as I am, what is left but to possess Thee without seeing Thee?

Ah, should I not rejoice at having that most extreme mercy and favour of possessing Thee at all? It is sin that has reduced me to live by faith, as I must at best, and should I not rejoice in such a life, O Lord my God? I see and know, O my good Jesus, that the only way in which I can possibly approach Thee in this world is the way of faith, faith in what Thou hast told me, and I thankfully follow this only way which Thou hast given me.

II. O my God, Thou dost over-abound in mercy! To live by faith is my necessity, from my present state of being and from my sin; but Thou hast pronounced a blessing on it. Thou hast said that I am more blessed if I believe on Thee, than if I saw Thee. Give me to share that blessedness, give it to me in its fulness. Enable me to believe as if I saw; let me have Thee always before me as if Thou wert always bodily and sensibly present. Let me ever hold communion with Thee, my hidden, but my living God.

Thou art in my innermost heart. Thou art the life of my life. Every breath I breathe, every thought of my mind, every good desire of my heart, is from the presence within me of the unseen God. By nature and by grace Thou art in me. I see Thee not in the material world except dimly, but I recognise Thy voice in my own intimate consciousness. I turn round and say Rabboni. O be ever thus with me; and if I am tempted to leave Thee, do not Thou, O my God, leave me!

III. O my dear Saviour, would that I had any right to ask to be allowed to make reparation to Thee for all the unbelief of the world, and all the insults offered to Thy Name, Thy Word, Thy Church, and the Sacrament of Thy Love! But, alas, I have a long score of unbelief and ingratitude of my own to atone for. Thou art in the Sacrifice of the Mass, Thou art in the Tabernacle, verily and indeed, in flesh and blood; and the world not only disbelieves, but mocks at this gracious truth.

Thou didst warn us long ago by Thyself and by Thy Apostles that Thou wouldst hide Thyself from the world. The prophecy is fulfilled more than ever now; but I know what the world knows not. O accept my homage, my praise, my adoration! Let me at least not be found wanting. I cannot help the sins of others – but one at least of those whom Thou hast redeemed shall turn round and with a loud voice glorify God. The more men scoff, the more will I believe in Thee, the good God, the good Jesus, the hidden Lord of life, who hast done me nothing else but good from the very first moment that I began to live.

3. Jesus the Light of the Soul
Stay with us, because it is towards evening.
I. I adore Thee, O my God, as the true and only Light! From Eternity to Eternity, before any creature was, when Thou wast alone, alone but not solitary, for Thou hast ever been Three in One, Thou wast

the Infinite Light. There was none to see Thee but Thyself. The Father saw that Light in the Son, and the Son in the Father.

Such as Thou wast in the beginning, such Thou art now. Most separate from all creatures in this Thy uncreated Brightness. Most glorious, most beautiful. Thy attributes are so many separate and resplendent colours, each as perfect in its own purity and grace as if it were the sole and highest perfection. Nothing created is more than the very shadow of Thee. Bright as are the Angels, they are poor and most unworthy shadows of Thee. They pale and look dim and gather blackness before Thee. They are so feeble beside Thee, that they are unable to gaze upon Thee. The highest Seraphim veil their eyes, by deed as well as by word proclaiming Thy unutterable glory.

For me, I cannot even look upon the sun, and what is this but a base material emblem of Thee? How should I endure to look even on an Angel? And how could I look upon Thee and live? If I were placed in the illumination of Thy countenance, I should shrink up like the grass. O most gracious God, who shall approach Thee, being so glorious, yet how can I keep from Thee?

II. How can I keep from Thee? For Thou, who art the Light of Angels, art the only Light of my soul. Thou enlightenest every man that cometh into this world. I am utterly dark, as dark as hell, without Thee.

I droop and shrink when Thou art away. I revive only in proportion as Thou dawnest upon me. Thou comest and goest at Thy will. O my God, I cannot keep Thee! I can only beg of Thee to stay. '*Mane nobiscum, Domine, quoniam advesperascit.*' Remain till morning, and then go not without giving me a blessing. Remain with me till death in this dark valley, when the darkness will end. Remain, O Light of my soul, *iam advesperascit!*

The gloom, which is not Thine, falls over me. I am nothing. I have little command of myself. I cannot do what I would. I am disconsolate and sad. I want something, I know not what. It is Thou that I want, though I so little understand this. I say it and take it on faith; I partially understand it, but very poorly. Shine on me, 'O fire ever burning and never failing' – and I shall begin, through and in Thy Light, to see Light, and to recognise Thee truly, as the Source of Light. *Mane nobiscum*; stay, sweet Jesus, stay for ever. In this decay of nature, give more grace.

III. Stay with me, and then I shall begin to shine as Thou shinest: so to shine as to be a light to others. The light, O Jesus, will be all from Thee. None of it will be mine. No merit to me. It will be Thou who shinest through me upon others. O let me thus praise Thee, in the way which Thou dost love best, by shining on all those around me.

Give light to them as well as to me; light them with me, through me. Teach me to show forth Thy praise, Thy truth, Thy will. Make me preach Thee without preaching – not by words, but by my example and by the catching force, the sympathetic influence, of what I do – by my visible resemblance to Thy saints, and the evident fulness of the love which my heart bears to Thee.

The emotional exclamatory style of the Meditations and Devotions *by John Henry Newman (1801–90) is characteristic of his age, but differs markedly from the style of his autobiographical, historical or theological works. They were published in book form after his death.*

13

Faith, hope and love

The Apostles' Creed
Traditional

I believe in God the Father Almighty,
Creator of heaven and earth;
and in Jesus Christ his only Son our Lord,
who was conceived by the Holy Ghost,
born of the Virgin Mary;
suffered under Pontius Pilate,
was crucified, dead, and buried;
he descended into hell,
the third day he rose again from the dead;
he ascended into heaven,
and sitteth on the right hand of God the Father Almighty;
from thence he shall come to judge the quick and the dead.
I believe in the Holy Ghost;
the holy Catholic Church;
the communion of saints;
the forgiveness of sins;
the resurrection of the body,
and the life everlasting. Amen.

*The contents of this creed are found as early as the writings of Tertullian (about
AD 200), even down to the reference to Pontius Pilate, as a means of historical
dating. Though the beliefs indeed come down from apostolic times, the associa-
tion was taken further in the Middle Ages by a popular attribution of each of
the twelve clauses in the creed to one of the twelve Apostles. Other creeds, such
as the so-called Nicene Creed, have refined the propositions concerning the
Trinity and Jesus, but the Apostles' Creed is still used in worship, for example
in the Book of Common Prayer's services of Baptism, both for infants and for
those of riper years. Although, according to the common teaching of Christianity, faith is one of the theological virtues, like hope and love, which cannot be
augmented merely by repetition, the prayerful recitation of the creeds constitutes
an act of faith, and disposes the believer to accept the grace of the virtue.*

An act of hope
John Gother

Thou hast prepared, O Lord, everlasting happiness for those that
love thee.
But how can I expect a part in this reward, who am a grievous
sinner and from my childhood have done evil in thy sight?
Ah, my God, while I look on myself I am terrified with my sins,
and see there nothing but reasons for despair;
and from this sense of my own unworthiness, I here declare I have
nothing of my own to trust to.
No, my God, nothing of my own, but all my hope is in thee.
I am dust and ashes,
but behold I offer to thee the passion and blood of thy only Son.
In that I have an infinite treasure of mercy stored up for me.
He laid down his life for sinners,
and became a propitiation for my offences.
It is this I now present to thee.
It is in this and thy promises I ground all my hope.
And since I have this to depend on, I will never despair but ever
preserve a firm and lively trust in thee.
Our Lord is my light and salvation, whom shall I fear?
Our Lord is my protector, and nothing shall hurt me.
Our Lord is merciful and full of compassion.
As a tender father has compassion on his children, so will our Lord
shew mercy to all that fear him;
for he knows what we are, and of what we are made.
He is sweet and tender to all,
and his mercies are above all this works.
He gives strength to the weak,
raises up those that fall,
comforts the afflicted,
and pardons sinners.
O God, all these good effects I hope thou wilt at present work in
my soul,
and so watch over me that nothing necessary to my salvation be
wanting to me.

John Gother died in 1704, and the seventeenth century was one in which English-speaking people shared a strong awareness of sin and the helplessness of humanity to achieve any friendship with God by their own efforts. Gother was a realistic and compassionate pastor who encouraged his people – servants, labourers, housewives, shopkeepers, clerks, traders, seafarers, farmers and prisoners – to turn with confidence to God.

Comfort and hope
Book of Common Prayer

A Prayer for persons troubled in mind or in conscience
O Blessed Lord, the Father of mercies, and the God of all comforts:
We beseech thee, look down in pity and compassion upon this thy
    afflicted servant.
Thou writest bitter things against him,
and makest him to possess his former iniquities;
thy wrath lieth hard upon him, and his soul is full of trouble:
But, O merciful God, who hast written thy holy Word for our
    learning,
that we, through patience and comfort of thy holy Scriptures,
    might have hope;
give him a right understanding of himself, and of thy threats and
    promises;
that he may neither cast away his confidence in thee,
nor place it any where but in thee.
Give him strength against all his temptations, and heal all his
    distempers.
Break not the bruised reed, nor quench the smoking flax.
Shut not up thy tender mercies in displeasure;
but make him to hear of joy and gladness,
that the bones which thou hast broken may rejoice.
Deliver him from fear of the enemy,
and lift up the light of thy countenance upon him, and give him
    peace,
through the merits and mediation of Jesus Christ our Lord. Amen.

(From the Order for the Visitation of the Sick)

St Francis's plank
Lady Lucy Herbert

Aspirations

Tu es, Domine, spes mea – You are, O Lord, my only hope.

In verbum tuum superspera vi – In your word I have hoped above all.

Etiam si occiderit me in ipso sperabo, et ipse erit Salvator meus – Although you should afflict me with all evils and should kill me, yet I will not cease to hope in you, my God and Saviour.

Non timebo mala quonian tu mecum es – I will fear no evil, because you, Lord, are with me.

Dominus regit me et nihil mihi deerit – Our Lord governs me and has care of me, and nothing shall be wanting to me.

And with St Francis, when he floated upon a plank in the sea: What have I to fear? God sees me and can help me. I will whatever He pleases.

Part of the spirituality practised by Lucy Herbert (1669–1744) entailed offering up to God short prayers or aspirations at odd moments during the day. This little collection of aspirations concerned with hope draws on reading that she had undertaken. She would have been familiar with the Bible in Latin, knowing the Psalms by heart. The sentence, 'Although you should afflict me with all evils and should kill me, yet I will not cease to hope in you', comes from the book of Job (13:15). St Francis of Assisi was shipwrecked when attempting to reach the Holy Land, about 1212.

God is where love is
The Missal

Ubi caritas et amor, Deus ibi est.
Congregavit nos in unum Christi amor.
Exultemus, et in ipso iucundemur.
Timeamus, et amemus Deum vivum.
Et ex corde diligamus nos sincero.

Where charity and love are, God is there.
Christ's love has gathered us into one.
Let us rejoice and be pleased in Him.
Let us fear, and let us love the living God.
And may we love each other with a sincere heart.

This is part of one of the antiphons sung during the ceremony of the Washing of the Feet at the Mass of the Last Supper on Maundy Thursday. The English rendering of caritas *in the Bible as 'charity' has been affected by the feebler meaning of charity as monetary donation to a good cause. But then 'love' has long been associated with profane romantic love, which may not be the image of God's love that it ideally can be. After all, the Prioress in the* Canterbury Tales *wears a brooch inscribed* 'Amor vincit omnia' *and Virgil in the* Eclogues *says* 'Omnia vincit amor et nos cedamus amori'. *Love as a theological virtue is a free gift of God.*

For charity
Book of Common Prayer

O Lord, who dost teach us that our doings without charity are nothing worth, send thy Holy Ghost and pour into our hearts that most excellent gift of charity, the very bond of peace and all virtues, without the which whosoever liveth is counted dead before thee; grant this for thy only Son Jesus Christ's sake. Amen.

(Collect for the Sunday Called Quinquagesima)

Wants and love
Thomas Traherne

Wants are the Bands and Cements between God and us.
Had we not Wanted,
we could never have been Obliged.
Whereas now we are infinitely Obliged,
because we Want infinitely.
From Eternity it was requisite that we should Want.

We could never else have Enjoyed any Thing:
Our own Wants are Treasures.
And if Want be a Treasure, sure every Thing is so.
Wants are the Ligatures between God and us.
The Sinews that convey Sences from him into us:
whereby we live in Him, and feel his Enjoyments.
For had we not been Obliged by having our Wants Satisfied,
we should not have been created to love Him.
And had we not been Created to love Him,
we could never have Enjoyed his Eternal Blessedness.

Love has a marvellous Property of feeling in another.
It can Enjoy in another, as well as Enjoy Him.
Love is an infinite Treasure to its Object,
and its Object is so to it.
GOD is LOVE, and you are His Object.
You are Created to be his Love;
and He is yours.
He is Happy in you, when you are Happy; as Parents in
    their Children.
He is Afflicted in all your Afflictions.
And whosoever toucheth you toucheth the Apple of His Eye.
Will not you be happy in all his Enjoyments?
He feeleth in you, will not you feel in Him?
He hath Obliged you to love Him.
And if you love Him you must of necessity be Heir of the
    world,
for you are Happy in Him.
All His Praises are your Joys,
all his Enjoyments are your Treasures,
all His Pleasures are your Enjoyments.
In GOD you are Crowned,
in GOD you are concerned.
In Him you feel,
in Him you live, and move and have your Being,
in Him you are Blessed.
Whatsoever therefore serveth Him serveth you
and in Him you inherit all Things.

These are numbers 51 and 52 in the First Century of Meditations *by Thomas Traherne (1637–74). Psalm 17, verse 8 says: 'Keep me as the apple of the eye', apple meaning 'pupil'. It was St Paul, in his address to the men of Athens on the Hill of Mars, who spoke of the one that they called the Unknown God: 'In him we live, and move, and have our being; as certain also of your own poets have said, For we are also his offspring' (Acts 17:28).*

Neutrality loathsome
Robert Herrick

God will have all, or none; serve Him or fall
Down before Baal, Bel or Belial:
Either be hot, or cold: God doth despise,
Abhorre, and spew out all Neutralities.

From Noble Numbers *by Robert Herrick (1591–1674). He refers to the passage in Revelation 3:15, where the message to the church of the Laodiceans is 'I know thy works, that thou art neither cold nor hot: I would thou wert cold or hot. So then because thou art lukewarm, and neither cold nor hot, I will spue thee out of my mouth.'*

Kindness
Jane Austen

Give us grace to endeavour after a truly Christian spirit to seek to attain that temper of forbearance and patience of which our blessed saviour has set us the highest example; and which, while it prepares us for the spiritual happiness of the life to come, will secure to us the best enjoyment of what this world can give. Incline us oh God! to think humbly of ourselves, to be severe only in the examination of our own conduct, to consider our fellow-creatures with kindness, and to judge of all they say and do with that charity which we would desire from them ourselves.

This extract is from an evening prayer by Jane Austen (1775–1817). The novelist's sharp powers of observation did not prevent her from seeking a more charitable attitude.

Our pattern
Jeremy Taylor

Full of mercy, full of love,
Look upon us from above,
Thou who taught'st the blind man's night
To entertain a double light,
Thine and the day's (and that thine too):
The lame away his crutches threw,
The parched crust of leprosy
Returned unto its infancy:
The dumb amazed was to hear
His own unchained tongue strike his ear;
The powerful mercy did even chase
The Devil from his usurped place,
Where thou thyself shouldst dwell, not he.

O let thy love our pattern be;
Let thy mercy teach one brother
To forgive and love another,
That copying thy mercy here,
Thy goodness may hereafter rear
Our souls unto thy glory, when
Our dust shall cease to be with men. Amen.

Although Jeremy Taylor (1613–67) ended up as Bishop of Down and Connor, in Ireland, he spent most of his life in England and Wales and much of it in adversity, because of the Civil War and the harsh treatment of Church of England clergy, especially those of a traditional outlook like his own. He found refuge as chaplain to the Carbery household at Golden Grove (Gelli-aur), a few miles south-west of Llandeilo and to the east of Carmarthen. Here he wrote his best known books, Holy Living *(1650), and* Holy Dying *(1651), as well as two volumes of sermons.*

Lovest thou me?

William Cowper

Hark, my soul, it is the Lord!
'Tis thy Saviour, hear his Word;
Jesus speaks, and speaks to thee,
'Say, poor sinner, lovest thou me?'

'I delivered thee when bound,
And, when bleeding, healed thy wound;
Sought thee wandering, set thee right,
Turned thy darkness into light.

'Can a woman's tender care
Cease toward the child she bare?
Yes, she may forgetful be,
Yet will I remember thee.

'Mine is an unchanging love,
Higher than the heights above,
Deeper than the depths beneath,
Free and faithful, strong as death.

'Thou shalt see my glory soon,
When the work of grace is done;
Partner of my throne shalt be:
Say, poor sinner, lovest thou me?'

Lord, it is my chief complaint
That my love is weak and faint;
Yet I love thee, and adore:
O for grace to love thee more!

By William Cowper (1731–1800), published in 1768 and included in Olney Hymns *(1779). It is in* Hymns Ancient and Modern *and* The Methodist Hymn Book.

God in the poor
Christina Rossetti

Behold, I stand at the door, and knock: if any man hear My Voice,
and open the door, I will come in to him, and will sup with him,
and he with Me. (Revelation 3:20)

O Lord Jesus Christ, Who standest at the door and knockest,
give us wisdom, I entreat Thee, to open our hearts wide unto
   Thee,
that Thou mayest enter in to abide and sup with us.
Grant us grace to discern and love Thee in Thy poor:
and according as Thou shalt call us,
to feed Thee in the hungry,
refresh Thee in the thirsty,
clothe Thee in the naked,
visit Thee in the sick,
comfort Thee in the prisoner,
receive Thee in the stranger,
bury that which is made after Thine Image in the dead. Amen.

The list of good works to others, given in this extract from Annus Domini *by
Christina Rossetti (1830–94), comes from Matthew 25:34 where, at the last
judgment, 'the King say unto them on his right hand, Come, ye blessed of my
Father, inherit the kingdom prepared for you from the foundation of the world:
For I was an hungred, and ye gave me meat: I was thirsty, and ye gave me
drink: I was a stranger, and ye took me in: Naked, and ye clothed me: I was
sick, and ye visited me: I was in prison, and ye came unto me. Then shall the
righteous answer him, saying, Lord, when saw we thee an hungred, and fed
thee? Or thirsty, and gave thee drink? When saw we thee a stranger, and took
thee in? Or naked, and clothed thee? Or when saw we thee sick, or in prison,
and came unto thee? And the King shall answer and say unto them, Verily I
say unto you, Inasmuch as ye have done it unto one of the least of these my
brethren, ye have done it unto me.' The burial of the dead, recognized as a
work of charity in, for example, the book of Tobit, is traditionally counted as
one of the seven corporal works of mercy.*

Fruit
Mother Teresa

The fruit of silence
is prayer
the fruit of prayer
is faith
the fruit of faith
is love
the fruit of love
is service
the fruit of service
is peace.

Mother Teresa of Calcutta (1910–97) founded the Missionaries of Charity to work with the poorest of the poor, in whom they were to see Jesus.

14
Daily life

Important hours
Jane Austen

Father of Heaven! whose goodness has brought us in safety to
the close of this day,
dispose our hearts in fervent prayer.
Another day is now gone, and added to those, for which we
were before accountable.
Teach us almighty Father, to consider this solemn truth, as we
should do,
that we may feel the importance of every day,
and every hour as it passes,
and earnestly strive to make a better use of what thy goodness
may yet bestow on us,
than we have done of the time past.

From an evening prayer by Jane Austen (1775–1817).

Save us, now
Book of Common Prayer

Lord, be merciful to us sinners, and save us for thy mercy's sake.

Thou art the great God, that hast made and rulest all things: O
deliver us for thy Name's sake.

Thou art the great God to be feared above all: O save us, that we
may praise thee.

*This is from one of the less visited portions of the Book of Common Prayer, the
'Short Prayers for single persons, that cannot meet to join in Prayer with
others, by reason of the Fight, or Storm'.*

One step enough
John Henry Newman

Lead, kindly Light, amid the encircling gloom,
Lead thou me on!
The night is dark, and I am far from home –
Lead thou me on!
Keep thou my feet; I do not ask to see
the distant scene – one step enough for me.

I was not ever thus, nor prayed that thou
Shouldst lead me on.
I loved to choose and see my path; but now
Lead thou me on!
I loved the garish day, and, spite of fears,
Pride ruled my will: remember not past years!

So long thy power hath blessed me, sure it still
Will lead me on,
O'er moor and fen, o'er crag and torrent, till
The night is gone;
And with the morn those angel faces smile,
Which I have loved long since, and lost awhile!

John Henry Newman (1801–90) was in Sicily in 1833 when he was struck down with fever. In his autobiographical book, the Apologia, *he recounts what happened next: 'My servant thought that I was dying, and begged for my last directions. I gave them, as he wished; but I said, "I shall not die." I repeated, "I shall not die, for I have not sinned against light, I have not sinned against light." I never have been able quite to make out what I meant. I got to Castro-Giovanni, and was laid up there for nearly three weeks. Towards the end of May I left for Palermo, taking three days for the journey. Before starting from my inn in the morning of May 26th or 27th, I sat down on my bed, and began to sob bitterly. My servant, who had acted as my nurse, asked what ailed me. I could only answer him, "I have a work to do in England." I was aching to get home; yet for want of a vessel I was kept at Palermo for three weeks . . . At last I got off in an orange boat, bound for Marseilles. Then it was that I wrote the lines, "Lead, kindly light", which have since become well known. We were becalmed a whole week in the Straits of*

Bonifacio . . . At last I got off again, and did not stop night or day (except a compulsory delay at Paris) till I reached England. The following Sunday, July 14th, Mr Keble preached the Assize Sermon in the University Pulpit. It was published under the title of "National Apostasy". I have ever considered and kept the day, as the start of the religious movement of 1833.' This is better known today as the Oxford Movement. But, prescinding from Newman's own adventures and his own life's work, the hymn has been much valued as an expression of the Christian's trust in God before the unknown future.

Against perils
Book of Common Prayer

From lightning and tempest; from earthquake, fire, and flood; from plague, pestilence, and famine; from battle and murder, and from sudden death,
    Good Lord, deliver us.

(From the Litany)

God's power
Anonymous

I bind to myself today
The strong virtue of the Invocation of the Trinity:
I believe the Trinity in the Unity
The Creator of the Universe.

I bind to myself today
The virtue of the Incarnation of Christ with His Baptism,
The virtue of His crucifixion with His burial,
The virtue of His Resurrection with His Ascension,
The virtue of His coming on the Judgement Day.

I bind to myself today
The virtue of the love of seraphim,
In the obedience of angels,

In the hope of resurrection unto reward,
In prayers of Patriarchs,
In predictions of Prophets,
In preaching of Apostles,
In faith of Confessors,
In purity of holy Virgins,
In deeds of righteous men.

I bind to myself today
The power of Heaven,
The light of the sun,
The brightness of the moon,
The splendour of fire,
The flashing of lightning,
The swiftness of wind,
The depth of sea,
The stability of earth,
The compactness of rocks.

I bind to myself today
God's Power to guide me,
God's Might to uphold me,
God's Wisdom to teach me,
God's Eye to watch over me,
God's Ear to hear me,
God's Word to give me speech,
God's Hand to guide me,
God's Way to lie before me,
God's Shield to shelter me,
God's Host to secure me,
Against the snares of demons,
Against the seductions of vices,
Against the lusts of nature,
Against everyone who meditates injury to me,
Whether far or near,
Whether few or with many.

I invoke today all these virtues
Against every hostile merciless power
Which may assail my body and my soul,
Against the incantations of false prophets,
Against the black laws of heathenism,
Against the false laws of heresy,
Against the deceits of idolatry,
Against the spells of women, and smiths, and druids,
Against every knowledge that binds the soul of man.

Christ, protect me today
Against every poison, against burning,
Against drowning, against death-wound,
That I may receive abundant reward.

Christ with me, Christ before me,
Christ behind me, Christ within me,
Christ beneath me, Christ above me,
Christ at my right, Christ at my left,
Christ in the fort,
Christ in the chariot seat,
Christ in the poop,
Christ in the heart of everyone who thinks of me,
Christ in the mouth of everyone who speaks to me,
Christ in every eye that sees me,
Christ in every ear that hears me.

I bind to myself today
The strong virtue of an invocation of the Trinity,
I believe the Trinity in the Unity
The Creator of the Universe.

This prayer is usually known as St Patrick's Breastplate (or Lorica, *the Latin for 'breastplate'). It is an old Irish prayer, perhaps from the eighth century. But St Patrick lived in the fifth century.*

The Captain
Christina Rossetti

It became Him, for Whom are all things, and by Whom are all things, in bringing many sons unto glory, to make the Captain of their Salvation perfect through sufferings. (Hebrews 2:10)

> O Lord Jesus Christ, Captain of our Salvation,
> help us, I pray Thee, always to bear in mind our vows,
> and to fight manfully under the banner of Thy Cross
> against the world, the flesh and the devil.
> By Thy Sufferings sanctify our sufferings;
> in Thy Strength make us stronger than our enemies;
> by virtue of Thy Victory give us victory. Amen.

From Annus Domini *by Christina Rossetti (1830–94).*

After a quarrel
The Seafarers' Prayer Book

O God, you know that today I have broken your commandment of
  love,
and that I have parted with my brother in anger.
Even if I have been wronged and insulted, teach me how to forgive.
Even if I was right, help me to make the first approach and to take
  the first step towards reconciliation.
Keep me from foolish pride and from nursing my foolish anger.
Help me to be thinking of Jesus, that in him I may see the example
  of how to forgive,
and that in him I may find the will and the power to forgive;
this I ask for your love's sake. Amen.

*One of the prayers in the prayer book published by the Apostleship of the Sea,
which works to support the faith of seafarers and their families in Britain and
round the world.*

An instrument

Anonymous

Lord make me an instrument of your peace

Where there is hatred,
Let me sow love;
Where there is injury, pardon;
Where there is doubt, faith;
Where there is despair, hope;
Where there is darkness, light;
And where there is sadness, joy.

O Divine Master grant that I may
Not so much seek to be consoled
As to console;
To be understood,
As to understand;
To be loved as to love.
For it is in giving that we receive,
It is in pardoning that we are pardoned.
And it is in dying that we are
Born to eternal life. Amen.

This prayer is often thought to be by St Francis of Assisi, but it first appeared in France in 1912 in a spiritual magazine called La Clochette, *published by a pious group founded in 1901 by Father Esther Bouquerel (1855–1923). The prayer bore the title of 'Belle priere faire pendant la messe' ('A Beautiful Prayer to Say During the Mass'). Marquis Stanislas de La Rochethulon sent a copy to Pope Benedict XV in 1915, and it was published in* L'Osservatore Romano. *In about 1920, the prayer was printed by a French Franciscan priest on the back of an image of St Francis with the title 'Priere pour la paix'. An English translation appeared in 1936 in a book called* Living Courageously *by Kirby Page (1890–1957), who attributed it to Francis of Assisi.*

Martha, Martha
Robert Herrick

The repetition of the name made known
No other than Christ's full Affection.

From Noble Numbers *by Robert Herrick (1591–1674). In Luke 10:38 we find the passage: 'Now it came to pass, as they went, that Jesus entered into a certain village: and a certain woman named Martha received him into her house. And she had a sister called Mary, which also sat at Jesus' feet, and heard his word. But Martha was cumbered about much serving, and came to him, and said, Lord, dost thou not care that my sister hath left me to serve alone? bid her therefore that she help me. And Jesus answered and said unto her, Martha, Martha, thou art careful and troubled about many things: But one thing is needful: and Mary hath chosen that good part, which shall not be taken away from her.' Mary has been taken to stand for the contemplative life and Martha for the active Christian life.*

Grace before meals
Traditional

Bless us, O Lord, and these thy gifts
which we are about to receive from thy bounty
through Christ our Lord. Amen.

The Latin version of this grace is said to date from the eighth century or earlier. It is used in several Oxford and Cambridge colleges, with varying additions.

A visit

William Walsham How

A prayer which may be said by the pastor on his way to a house of sickness

O good shepherd, Who camest to seek and to save that which
   was lost,
be with me in this my work.
Strengthen me in my weakness.
Give me greater zeal for Thy glory;
greater love for the souls Thou diedst to save.
Let not my sins or infirmities hinder Thy grace.
Grant me faithfulness with tenderness and boldness with
   meekness.
Teach me, that I may teach.
Comfort me, that I may comfort.
Bless that which I shall speak in Thy Name.
And have mercy both upon the pastor and upon the flock;
for Thine own merits' sake. Amen.

Behold I stand at the door and knock.
Who is it who speaks these loving lowly words? Who is it who is standing there so humbly and patiently? I think I need not tell you. But
this I will tell you, that He is standing now knocking at the door of
your heart.

Your sickness is the knocking of His gentle Hand.

What does He want? That also I think you know. He wants to be
taken into your heart. He wants to find an entrance there, that He
may pass in, and stay with you, and give you all his best and richest
blessings. What a wonderful thing it is that He should wish to find a
home in such a poor cold bare place as your heart must seem to
Him! Yes, it is a wonderful thing; but it is true.

This is not the first time He has knocked by a great many. Oh, how
patient He is! Why has He not gone away long ago, when He found
you would not open the door? It is only because He loves you so
greatly that He will not go away till there is no more hope.

Oh how blind we are that we see not the blessed Form that
is seeking to come in, – that is standing there, in such wondrous

humility, His Hands pierced with the nails, His Side rent with the spear, – that lowly Form, standing there, outside, waiting – most patiently waiting – till we will open the door and let Him in!

Oh how deaf we are that we hear not the pleading accents of that loving, gentle Voice, so meekly begging to enter! 'Behold,' it saith, – 'Behold, I stand at the door and knock.'

Shame upon us to keep Him waiting there so long! Is this the way to treat Him? Is this the way to behave to Him Who comes to us with such a longing desire to be let in that He may bring to us all the riches of His bounty and grace? What if it were some earthly mes-senger bringing us a handful of gold? Should we care so little then? Should we let *him* wait so long outside? Nay, I think we should run to the door, and open it wide, and ask him eagerly to come in. He would have a hearty welcome. But *This* One – this meek and lowly One, who is waiting there, knocking now and then, hoping to be admitted at last, – *This* is only JESUS – only our SAVIOUR, who gave His life for us.

He must wait. It is not worth while being in such a hurry to open the door for *Him*. He brings no gold in His Hand. He has only got heaven to offer. And heaven is far off. We do not think much of that. He must wait.

Am I not speaking true things? It is the truth (is it not?) that most of us would do more to welcome any one who came to us with a handful of gold, than we will to welcome Him who brings us heaven.

Perhaps you fancy that even if you were ready to open the door of your heart, yet He who has knocked there so often in vain, would never really cross the threshold. Oh, think it not. It is wronging His love to think it. I would that I had some power to open your soul's eye for a moment, that you might see Him standing there waiting – patiently waiting – till even *you* will let Him come in. *He* is ready. *He* is willing to enter. It is *you* who will not open the door. It is *you* who will not believe in His patience, and love, and forgiveness. You may have refused to let Him pass in again and again refused roughly, rudely, daringly. But He is standing there yet. He has not quite gone away. Once more you may, if you will, catch the pleading voice, 'Behold, I stand at the door and knock.' Oh shall it be *this time in vain*? No! It cannot – it shall not – be in vain.

JESUS, SAVIOUR, too long have we shut our ears to Thy Voice of mercy. Too long have we barred and bolted the door of our stubborn hearts against Thee. Now, yes now, full of sorrow, yet full of hope, with trembling hands, we open wide the door, and pray Thee, of Thine infinite compassion, to come in and abide with us, and never more to leave us or forsake us. Amen.

William Walsham How (1823–97) was Rector of Whittington, Shropshire, for 28 years, refusing a bishopric five times until in 1879 he agreed to become a suffragan bishop of London. He worked to improve the position of the poor in the East End. In 1889 he became the first Bishop of Wakefield. He wrote more than 50 hymns, of which the best known is 'For All the Saints'. In 1868 he published Pastor in Parochia, *a devotional manual for clergymen visiting their parishes. My own copy contains a manuscript rota drawn up for visiting mostly labourers and dock workers and their families at Gravesend on the Thames.*

In loneliness
The Seafarers' Prayer Book

O God, I came to you for comfort.
You know how lonely I am, O God,
keep me from living too much in the past.
Keep me from living too much in memories and too little with
    hopes.
Keep me from being too sorry for myself.
Help me to remember that I am going through what many
    another has gone through.
Help me not to sorrow as those who have no hope.
Help me to find comfort in my work,
and, because I have gone through sorrow myself, help me to
    help others who are in trouble.
This I ask for your love's sake. Amen.

This comes from the prayer book compiled by the Apostleship of the Sea.

No more lies

Susanna Wesley

What! Never speak one evil word!
Or rash, or idle, or unkind?
O! how shall I, most gracious Lord,
This mark of true perfection find?
Thy sinless mind in me reveal;
Thy Spirit's plenitude impart;
And all my spotless life shall tell
The abundance of Thy loving heart.

Enable me, O God, to keep a due regard over my words, that I may habitually speak nothing but what is true on all occasions.

Show me what a high offence it is against the God of Truth to speak falsely, either through design or inadvertence.

In telling any story or relating past actions may I be careful to speak deliberately and calmly, avoiding immoderate mirth or scornful laughter on the one hand and uncharitableness and excessive anger on the other, lest invention supply the defect of my memory.

May I ever remember that I am in the presence of the great and holy God, and that every sin is a contradiction and offence to some divine attribute, and that lying is opposite and offensive to Thy truth. Amen

The prayer by Susanna Wesley (1669–1742, the formidable mother of John), acts as a commentary to one of the hymns used by Methodists in the eighteenth century, published under John Wesley's editorship, and republished in the nineteenth century.

For self-forgetfulness
Robert Louis Stevenson

Lord, the creatures of thy hand, thy disinherited children,
come before thee with their incoherent wishes and regrets:
Children we are, children we shall be,
till our mother the earth hath fed upon our bones.
Accept us, correct us, guide us, thy guilty innocents.
Dry our vain tears, wipe out our vain resentments, help our yet
   vainer efforts.
If there be any here, sulking as children will, deal with and
   enlighten him.
Make it day about that person, so that he shall see himself and
   be ashamed.
Make it heaven about him, Lord, by the only way to heaven,
   forgetfulness of self,
and make it day about his neighbours, so that they shall help,
   not hinder him.

Robert Louis Stevenson (1850–94) spent the last four years of his life with his family at a plantation of Vailima, in Samoa, high above the Pacific. He wrote: 'In every Samoan household the day is closed with prayer and the singing of hymns. The omission of this sacred duty would indicate, not only a lack of religious training in the house chief, but a shameless disregard of all that is reputable in Samoan social life.'

15

Morning and night

This day
Lancelot Andrewes

Litany
Glory be to Thee, O Lord, glory to Thee.
Glory to Thee who givest me sleep
to recruit my weakness,
and to remit the toils
of this fretful flesh.
To this day and all days
a perfect, holy, peaceful, healthy, sinless course,
Vouchsafe O Lord.

The Angel of peace, a faithful guide,
Guardian of souls and bodies,
to encamp around me,
and ever to prompt what is salutary,
Vouchsafe O Lord.

Pardon and remission
of all sins and of all offences
Vouchsafe O Lord.

To our souls what is good and convenient,
And peace to the world
Vouchsafe O Lord.

Repentance and strictness
for the residue of our life,
and health and peace to the end,
Vouchsafe O Lord.

Whatever is true, whatever is honest,
whatever just, whatever pure,
whatever lovely, whatever of good report,
if there be any virtue, if any praise,
such thoughts, such deeds,
Vouchsafe O Lord.

A Christian close,
without sin, without shame,
and, should it please Thee, without pain,
and a good answer
at the dreadful and fearful judgement-seat
of Jesus Christ our Lord,
Vouchsafe O Lord.

Confession
Essence beyond essence, Nature increate,
Framer of the world,
I set Thee, Lord, before my face,
and I lift up my soul unto Thee.
I worship Thee on my knees,
and humble myself under Thy mighty hand.
I stretch forth my hands unto Thee,
My soul graspeth unto Thee as a thirsty Land.
I smite on my breast
and say with the Publican,
God be merciful to me a sinner,
the chief of sinners;
to the sinner above the Publican,
be merciful as to the Publican.
Father of mercies,
I beseech Thy fatherly affection.
Despise me not
an unclean worm, a dead dog, a putrid corpse,
despise not Thou the work of Thine own hands,
despise not Thine own image
though branded by sin.
Lord, if Thou wilt, Thou canst make me clean,
Lord, only say the word, and I shall be cleansed.
And Thou, my Saviour Christ,

Christ my Saviour,
Saviour of sinners, of whom I am chief,
despise me not, despise me not, O Lord,
despise not the cost of Thy blood,
who am called by Thy Name;
but look on me with those eyes
with which Thou didst look upon
Magdalene at the feast,
Peter in the hall,
The thief on the wood: –
That with the thief I may entreat Thee humbly,
Remember me, Lord, in Thy kingdom;
That with Peter I may bitterly weep and say,
O that mine eyes were a fountain of tears
that I might weep day and night;
that with Magdalene I may hear Thee say,
Thy sins be forgiven thee,
and with her may love much,
for many sins yea manifold
have been forgiven me.
And Thou, All-holy, Good, and Life-giving Spirit,
despise me not, Thy breath,
despise not Thine own holy things;
but turn Thee again, O Lord, at the last,
and be gracious unto Thy servant.

Commendation
Blessed art Thou, O Lord,
Our God,
the God of our Fathers;
Who turnest the shadow of death into the morning;
And lightenest the face of the earth;
Who separatest darkness from the face of the light;
and banishest night and bringest back the day;
Who lightenest mine eyes,
that I sleep not in death;
Who deliverest me from the terror by night,
from the pestilence that walketh in darkness;
Who drivest sleep from mine eyes,
And slumber from mine eyelids;

Who makest the outgoings of the morning and evening
to praise Thee;
because I laid me down and slept and rose up again,
for the Lord sustained me;
because I waked and beheld,
and my sleep was sweet unto me.
Blot out as a thick cloud my transgressions,
And as a cloud my sins;
grant me to be a child of light, a child of the day,
to walk soberly, holily, honestly, as in the day,
vouchsafe to keep me this day without sin.
Thou who upholdest the falling and liftest the fallen,
let me not harden my heart in provocation,
or temptation or deceitfulness of any sin.
Moreover, deliver me to-day
from the snare of the hunter
and from the noisome pestilence;
from the arrow that flieth by day,
from the sickness that destroyeth in the noon day.
Defend this day against my evil,
against the evil of this day defend Thou me.
Let not my days be spent in vanity,
Nor my years in sorrow,
One day telleth another,
And one night certifieth another.
O let me hear Thy loving-kindness betimes in the
    morning,
for in Thee is my trust;
shew Thou me the way that I should walk in,
for I lift up my soul unto Thee.
Deliver me, O Lord, from mine enemies,
for I flee unto Thee.
Teach me to do the thing that pleaseth Thee,
for Thou art my God;
let Thy loving Spirit lead me forth
into the land of righteousness.
Quicken me, O Lord, for Thy Name's sake,
And for Thy righteousness' sake
bring my soul out of trouble;
remove from me foolish imaginations,

inspire those which are good
and pleasing in Thy sight.
Turn away mine eyes
lest they behold vanity;
let mine eyes look right on,
and let mine eyelids look straight before me.
Hedge up mine ears with thorns
lest they incline to undisciplined words.
Give me early the ear to hear,
and open mine ears to the instruction of Thy oracles.
Set a watch, O Lord, before my mouth,
and keep the door of my lips.
Let my word be seasoned with salt,
that it may minister grace to the hearers.
Let no deed be grief unto me
nor offence of heart.
Let me do some work
for which Thou wilt remember me, Lord, for good,
and spare me according to the greatness of Thy mercy.
Into Thine hands I commend
my spirit, soul, and body,
which Thou hast created, redeemed, regenerated,
O Lord, Thou God of truth;
And together with me
All mine and all that belongs to me.
Thou hast vouchsafed them to me,
Lord, in Thy goodness.
Guard us from all evil,
guard our souls,
I beseech Thee, O Lord.
Guard us without falling,
and place us immaculate
in the presence of Thy glory
in that day.
Guard my going out and my coming in
henceforth and for ever.
Prosper, I pray Thee, Thy servant this day,
and grant him mercy
in the sight of those who meet him.
O God, make speed to save me,

O Lord, make haste to help me.
O turn Thee then unto me,
and have mercy upon me;
give Thy strength unto Thy servant,
and help the son of Thine handmaid.
Show some token upon me for good,
that they who hate me may see it and be ashamed,
because Thou, Lord, hast holpen me and comforted me.

This exercise in morning prayer by Lancelot Andrewes (1555–1626), found in his Preces Privatae, *reflects his methodical approach and scriptural learning. The translation from the Greek in which it was written is by John Henry Newman.*

The morning-watch
Henry Vaughan

O joys! Infinite sweetness ! with what flowers
And shoots of glory, my soul breaks and buds!
  All the long hours
  Of night and rest,
  Through the still shrouds
  Of sleep, and clouds,
 This dew fell on my breast;
  O how it bloods,
And spirits all my earth! hark! in what rings,
And hymning circulations the quick world
  Awakes, and sings!
  The rising winds,
  And falling springs,
  Birds, beasts, all things
 Adore Him in their kinds.
  Thus all is hurl'd
In sacred hymns and order; the great chime
And symphony of Nature.

Henry Vaughan (1621–95), from Silex Scintillans, *the collection that he compiled in the 1650s.*

Dawn

Liturgy of the Hours

Lux ecce surgit aurea.

See, the golden dawn is glowing,
While the paly shades are going,
Which have led us far and long,
In a labyrinth of wrong.

May it bring us peace serene;
May it cleanse, as it is clean;
Plain and clear our words be spoke,
And our thoughts without a cloak;

So the day's account, shall stand.
Guileless tongue and holy hand,
Stedfast eyes and unbeguiled,
'Flesh as of a little child.'

There is One who from above
Watches how the still hours move
Of our day of service done,
From the dawn to setting sun.

To the Father, and the Son,
And the Spirit, Three and One,
As of old, and as in Heaven,
Now and here be glory given.

This hymn for Lauds on Thursdays is from a series of free translations from the Breviary made in 1836–38 by John Henry Newman (1801–90).

Night prayer
Alcuin

May he, who with a calm mind slept in the stern,
Then got up and commanded the winds and the sea,
Grant that, while my limbs rest here, weary with heavy work,
My mind may keep vigil with him.
Lamb of God, who bore all the sins of the world,
Keep my calm rest safe from the enemy.

Alcuin (735–804), after his career in teaching, seems to have acquired a habit of prayerful serenity by the time he died in retirement at the Abbey of St Martin at Tours.

Lighten our darkness
Book of Common Prayer

Lighten our darkness, we beseech thee, O Lord, and by thy great mercy defend us from all perils and dangers of this night, for the love of thy only Son, our Saviour Jesus Christ. Amen.

(From the service of Evensong)

Family prayers
John Wesley

Monday evening
Almighty and most merciful Father,
in whom we live, move, and have our being;
to whose tender compassions we owe our safety the day past,
together with all the comforts of this life and the hopes of that
    which is to come;
we praise thee, O Lord, we bow ourselves before thee,
acknowledging we have nothing but what we receive from thee.
'Unto thee do we give thanks', O God,
who daily pourest thy benefits upon us.

Blessed be thy goodness for our health,
for our food and raiment,
for our peace and safety,
for the love of our friends,
for all our blessings in this life, and our desire to attain that life
which is immortal.
Blessed be thy love,
for that we feel in our hearts any motion toward thee.
Behold, O Lord, we present ourselves before thee,
to be inspired with such a vigorous sense of thy love,
as may put us forward with a greater earnestness, zeal, and
diligence in all our duty.
Renew in us, we beseech, a lively image of thee,
in all righteousness, purity, mercy, faithfulness, and truth.
O that Jesus, the hope of glory, may be formed in us,
in all humility, meekness, patience,
and an absolute surrender of our souls and bodies to thy holy will;
that we may not live, but Christ may live in us,
that every one of us may say, 'The life I now live in the flesh, I live
by faith in the Son of God, who loved me, and gave himself for
me.'
Let the remembrance of his love,
who made himself an offering for our sins,
be ever dear and precious to us.
Let it continually move us to offer up ourselves to thee,
to do thy will, as our blessed Master did.
May we place an entire confidence in thee,
and still trust ourselves with thee,
who hast not 'spared thine own Son, but freely given him up for us
all'.
May we humbly accept of whatsoever thou sendest us,
and 'in everything give thanks'.
Surely thou 'wilt never leave us nor forsake us'.
O guide us safe through all the changes of this life,
in an unchangeable love in thee,
and a lively sense of thy love to us,
till we come to live with thee and enjoy thee for ever.
And now that we are going to lay ourselves down to sleep,
take us into thy gracious protection,

and settle our spirits in such quiet and delightful thoughts of the
 glory where our Lord Jesus lives,
that we may desire to be dissolved and to go to him who died for us,
that, whether we wake or sleep, we might live together with him.
To thy blessing we recommend all mankind,
high and low, rich and poor,
that they may all faithfully serve thee,
and contentedly enjoy whatsoever is needful for them.
And especially we beseech thee, that the course of this world may
 be so peaceably ordered by thy governance,
that thy Church may joyfully serve thee in all godly quietness.
We leave all we have with thee,
especially our friends, and those who are dear unto us;
desiring that when we are dead and gone,
they may lift up their souls in this manner unto thee;
and teach those that come after, to praise, love, and obey thee.
And if we awake again in the morning,
may we praise thee again with joyful lips,
and still offer ourselves a more acceptable sacrifice to thee,
through Jesus Christ;
in whose words we beseech thee to hear us,
according to the full sense and meaning thereof:
'Our Father,' &c.

From Prayers for Families, *which provides similar prayers for each evening*
of the week, by John Wesley (1703–91), the great founder of Methodism.

A continuance of mercies
Jane Austen

We thank thee with all our hearts for every gracious
 dispensation,
for all the blessings that have attended our lives,
for every hour of safety, health and peace,
of domestic comfort and innocent enjoyment.
We feel that we have been blessed far beyond any thing that we
 have deserved;

and though we cannot but pray for a continuance of all these
    mercies,
we acknowledge our unworthiness of them
and implore thee to pardon the presumption of our desires.
Keep us oh! Heavenly Father from evil this night.
Bring us in safety to the beginning of another day
and grant that we may rise again with every serious and
    religious feeling which now directs us.
May thy mercy be extended over all mankind,
bringing the ignorant to the knowledge of thy truth,
awakening the impenitent,
touching the hardened.
Look with compassion upon the afflicted of every condition,
assuage the pangs of disease,
comfort the broken in spirit.

From an evening prayer by Jane Austen (1775–1817).

In wakefulness
The Seafarers' Prayer Book

O Lord, let me sleep:
You have said that you will give your beloved sleep.
I know you love me, please give me sleep.
Or let me rest quietly in you
and realise that I am sharing with you the sleeplessness of the
    starving, the lonely, the lost and the old
who are so much worse off than me.
Let me know that my wakefulness is not wasted
but helps to make up what is lacking in your suffering.

*From the prayer book published by the Apostleship of the Sea. The last line is
a reference to Colossians 1:23: 'I Paul am made a minister; Who now rejoice
in my sufferings for you, and fill up that which is behind of the afflictions of
Christ in my flesh for his body's sake, which is the church.'*

Shadows sink
Hannah More

Thy wisdom guides, Thy will directs
Thy hand upholds, Thy power protects;
With Thee when I at dawn converse,
The shadows sink, the clouds disperse.

From 'A Midnight Hymn' by Hannah More (1745–1833), who, after estab-
lishing her reputation as a bluestocking, as intellectual women were known,
succeeded in selling large numbers of the books she wrote on religious subjects,
particularly on the improvement of the way people acted. She was an orthodox
member of the Church of England, encouraged by the evangelical movement.
She was moved by her beliefs to undertake philanthropic works. The day before
she died, she was heard to shout out 'Joy!' It was her last word.

Unfathomable mines
William Cowper

God moves in a mysterious way
His wonders to perform;
He plants His footsteps in the sea
And rides upon the storm.

Deep in unfathomable mines
Of never failing skill
He treasures up His bright designs
And works His sovereign will.

Ye fearful saints, fresh courage take;
The clouds ye so much dread
Are big with mercy and shall break
In blessings on your head.

Judge not the Lord by feeble sense,
But trust Him for His grace;

Behind a frowning providence
He hides a smiling face.

His purposes will ripen fast,
Unfolding every hour;
The bud may have a bitter taste,
But sweet will be the flower.

Blind unbelief is sure to err
And scan His work in vain;
God is His own interpreter,
And He will make it plain.

*By William Cowper (1731–1800), first published in 1774, under the title
'Conflict. Light shining out of darkness'. It is included in both* Hymns
Ancient and Modern *and* The Methodist Hymn Book.

The evening
Lancelot Andrewes

Meditation
The day is gone,
and I give Thee Thanks, O Lord.
Evening is at hand,
make it bright unto us.
As day has its evening
so also has life;
the even of life is age,
age has overtaken me,
make it bright unto us.
Cast me not away in the time of age;
forsake me not when my strength faileth me.
Even to my old age be Thou He,
and even to hoar hairs carry me;
do Thou make, do Thou bear,
do Thou carry and deliver me.
Abide with me, Lord,

for it is toward evening,
and the day is far spent
of this fretful life.
Let Thy strength be made perfect
in my weakness.
Day is fled and gone,
life too is going,
this lifeless life.
Night cometh,
and cometh death,
the deathless death.
Near as is the end of day,
so too the end of life.
We then, also remembering it,
beseech of Thee
for the close of our life,
that Thou wouldest direct it in peace,
Christian, acceptable,
sinless, shameless,
and, if it please Thee, painless,
Lord, O Lord,
gathering us together
under the feet of Thine Elect,
when Thou wilt, and as Thou wilt,
only without shame and sins.
Remember we the days of darkness,
For they shall be many,
Lest we be cast into outer darkness.
Remember we to outstrip the night
doing some good thing.
Near is judgement –
a good and acceptable answer
at the dreadful and fearful judgement-seat
of Jesus Christ
vouchsafe to us, O Lord.
By night I lift up my hands in the sanctuary,
and praise the Lord.
The Lord hath granted His loving-kindness
in the day time;
and in the night season did I sing of Him,

and made my prayer unto the God of my life.
As long as I live will I magnify Thee on this manner,
and lift up my hands in Thy Name.
Let my prayer be set forth in Thy sight
as the incense,
and let the lifting up of my hands
be an evening sacrifice.
Blessed art Thou, O Lord, our God,
the God of our fathers,
who hast created the changes of days and nights,
who givest songs in the night,
who hast delivered us from the evil of this day,
who hast not cut off like a weaver my life,
nor from day even to night made an end of me.

Confession
Lord,
as we add day to day,
so sin to sin.
The just falleth seven times a day;
and I, an exceeding sinner,
seventy times seven;
a wonderful, a horrible thing, O Lord.
But I turn with groans
from my evil ways,
and I return into my heart,
and with all my heart I turn to Thee,
O God of penitents and Saviour of sinners;
and evening by evening I will return
in the innermost marrow of my soul;
and my soul out of the deep
crieth unto Thee.
I have sinned, O Lord, against Thee,
heavily against Thee;
alas, alas, woe is me! for my misery.
I repent, O me! I repent, spare me, O Lord,
I repent, O me, I repent,
help Thou my impenitence.
Be appeased, spare me, O Lord;
be appeased, have mercy on me;

I said, Lord, have mercy upon me;
heal my soul, for I have sinned against Thee.
Have mercy upon me, O Lord,
after Thy great goodness,
according to the multitude of Thy mercies
do away mine offences.
Remit the guilt,
heal the wound,
blot out the stains,
clear away the shame,
rescue from the tyranny,
and make me not a public example.
O bring Thou me out of my trouble,
cleanse Thou me from secret faults,
keep back Thy servant also from
presumptuous sins.
My wanderings of mind
and idle talking
lay not to my charge.
Remove the dark and muddy flood
of foul and wicked thoughts.
O Lord,
I have destroyed myself;
whatever I have done amiss, pardon mercifully.
Deal not with us after our sins,
neither reward us after our iniquities.
Look mercifully upon our infirmities;
and for the glory of Thy All-holy Name,
turn from us all those ills and miseries,
which by our sins, and by us through them,
are most righteously and worthily deserved.

Commendation
To my weariness, O Lord,
vouchsafe Thou rest,
to my exhaustion
renew Thou strength.
Lighten mine eyes that I sleep not in death.
Deliver me from the terror by night,
the pestilence that walketh in darkness.

Supply me with healthy sleep,
and to pass through this night without fear.
O keeper of Israel,
who neither slumberest nor sleepest,
guard me this night from all evil,
guard my soul, O Lord.
Visit me with the visitation of Thine own,
reveal to me wisdom in the visions of the night.
If not, for I am not worthy, not worthy,
at least, O loving Lord,
Let sleep be to me a breathing time
as from toil, so from sin.
Yea, O Lord,
nor let me in my dream imagine
what may anger Thee,
what may defile me.
Let not my loins be filled with illusions,
yea, let my reins chasten me in the night season,
yet without grievous terror.
Preserve me from the black sleep of sin;
all earthly and evil thoughts
put to sleep within me.
Grant to me light sleep,
rid of all imaginations
fleshly and satanical.
Lord, Thou knowest
how sleepless are mine unseen foes,
and how feeble my wretched flesh,
Who madest me;
shelter me with the wing of Thy pity;
awaken me at the fitting time,
the time of prayer;
and give me to seek Thee early,
for Thy glory and for Thy service.

Into Thy hands, O Lord, I commend myself,
my spirit, soul, and body:
Thou didst make, and didst redeem them;
and together with me, all my friends
and all that belongs to me.

Thou hast vouchsafed them to me, Lord,
in Thy goodness.
Guard my lying down and my rising up,
from henceforth and for ever.
Let me remember Thee on my bed,
and search out my spirit;
let me wake up and be present with Thee;
let me lay down in peace, and take my rest:
for it is Thou, Lord, only
that makest me dwell in safety.

This scheme for Evening Prayer comes from the Preces Privatae *of Lancelot Andrewes and matches the morning prayers at the beginning of this chapter. He concludes with the verse from Psalm 4 that so struck Augustine of Hippo (see Chapter 1).*

16

This life completed

Sure and certain hope
Book of Common Prayer

When they come to the Grave, while the Corpse is made ready to be laid into the earth, the Priest shall say, or the Priest and Clerks shall sing:

Man that is born of a woman hath but a short time to live, and is full of misery. He cometh up, and is cut down, like a flower; he fleeth as it were a shadow, and never continueth in one stay.

In the midst of life we are in death: of whom may we seek for succour, but of thee, O Lord, who for our sins art justly displeased?

Yet, O Lord God most holy, O Lord most mighty, O holy and most merciful Saviour, deliver us not into the bitter pains of eternal death.

Thou knowest, Lord, the secrets of our hearts; shut not thy merciful ears to our prayer; but spare us, Lord most holy, O God most mighty, O holy and merciful Saviour, thou most worthy judge eternal, suffer us not, at our last hour, for any pains of death, to fall from thee.

Then, while the earth shall be cast upon the Body by some standing by, the Priest shall say:

Forasmuch as it hath pleased Almighty God of his great mercy to take unto himself the soul of our dear brother here departed, we therefore commit his body to the ground; earth to earth, ashes to ashes, dust to dust; in sure and certain hope of the Resurrection to eternal life, through our Lord Jesus Christ; who shall change our vile body, that it may be like unto his glorious body, according to the mighty working, whereby he is able to subdue all things to himself.

(From the Burial Service)

Let me see Thy face
Augustine of Hippo

Oh! that I might repose on Thee!

Oh! that Thou wouldest enter into my heart, and inebriate it, that I
    may forget my ills, and embrace Thee, my sole good!

What art Thou to me? In Thy pity, teach me to utter it.

Or what am I to Thee that Thou demandest my love, and, if I give
    it not, art wroth with me, and threatenest me with grievous
    woes?

Is it then a slight woe to love Thee not?

Oh! for Thy mercies' sake, tell me, O Lord my God, what Thou art
    unto me.

Say unto my soul, I am thy salvation.

So speak, that I may hear.

Behold, Lord, my heart is before Thee;

open Thou the ears thereof, and say unto my soul, I am thy
    salvation.

After this voice let me haste, and take hold on Thee.

Hide not Thy face from me.

Let me die – lest I die – only let me see Thy face.

Once more, in his Confessions, *Augustine of Hippo (354–430) expostulates
with God and with himself.*

Repair me now
John Donne

Thou hast made me, and shall thy work decay?
Repair me now, for now mine end doth haste;
I run to death, and death meets me as fast,
And all my pleasures are like yesterday.
I dare not move my dim eyes any way;
Despair behind, and death before doth cast
Such terror, and my feebled flesh doth waste
By sin in it, which it towards hell doth weigh.

Only thou art above, and when towards thee
By thy leave I can look, I rise again;
But our old subtle foe so tempteth me
That not one hour I can myself sustain.
Thy grace may wing me to prevent his art,
And thou like adamant draw mine iron heart.

This is the first of the 'Holy Sonnets' by John Donne (1572–1631). The scholar Helen Gardner usefully points out that in the last line the word 'and' means 'if'.

Vain terrors

Samuel Johnson

Almighty and most merciful Father, before whom I now appear laden with the Sins of another year, suffer me yet again to call upon thee for pardon and peace.

O God, grant me repentance, grant me reformation.

Grant that I may be no longer disturbed with doubts and harassed with vain terrours. Grant that I may no more linger in perplexity, nor waste in idleness that life which thou hast given and preserved.

Grant that I may serve thee with firm faith and diligent endeavour, and that I may discharge the duties of my calling with tranquillity and constancy.

Take not O Lord thy Holy Spirit from me, but grant that I may so direct my life by thy holy laws, as that when thou shalt call me hence, I may pass by a holy and happy death to a life of everlasting and unchangeable joy, for the Sake of Jesus Christ, our Lord. Amen.

This prayer by Samuel Johnson (1709–84) was written on 29 March 1766. He had long been plagued by scruples and fears of death. When death came, eighteen years later, he met it with fortitude and peace of mind.

In the hour of death
Book of Common Prayer

In all time of our tribulation; in all time of our prosperity; in the hour of death, and in the day of judgement,
   Good Lord, deliver us.

(From the Litany)

No cold love
Thomas More

Before the feast of the pascha, Jesus, knowing that His hour came on to go out of this world unto His Father, whereas He had loved those that were His, unto the end He loved them. (John 13:1)

In these words the holy evangelist Saint John, whom Christ so tenderly loved that on His breast he leaned in His last supper, and to him secretly He uttered the false dissimuled traitor, and into whose custody He commended on the cross His own dear, heavy [sorrowful] mother, and which is (for the manifold tokens of Christ's special favour) specially called in the gospel, the disciple that Jesus loved, declareth here what a manner of faithful lover our holy Saviour was, of whom himself was so beloved.

For unto those words he putteth and forthwith joineth the rehearsing of His bitter passion, beginning with His maundy, and therein His humble washing of His disciples' feet, the sending forth of the traitor, and after that His doctrine, His prayer, His taking, His judging, His scourging, His crucifying, and all the whole piteous tragedy of His most bitter passion. Before all which things he setteth these fore-rehearsed words to declare that all these things that Christ did, in all this He did it for very love. Which love He well declared unto His disciples by many manner means at the time of His maundy, giving them in charge that in loving each other they should follow the example of Himself.

For He, those that He loved, He loved unto the end, and so would He that they should. He was not an unconstant lover that doth, as many do, love for a while and then upon a light occasion leave off and turn from a friend to an enemy, as the false traitor Judas did. But

He still so persevereth in love unto the very end, that for very love He came to that painful end; and yet not only for His friends that were already His, but for His enemies, to make them friends of His, and that not for His benefit but only for their own.

And here shall we note that, whereas the gospel saith in this place and divers other that Christ should go out of this world unto His Father (as where He said, 'Poor men shall ye alway have, but me shall you not alway have'), it is not meant that He shall be no more with His church here in the world nor come no more here till the day of doom. For Himself promised and said, 'I am with you all the days even unto the end of the world.' He is here in His Godhead, He is here in the blessed sacrament of the altar, and sundry times hath here, since His ascension, appeared unto divers holy men. But those other words, as Saint Hierome saith (and Saint Beda too), are understanden that He will not be here in corporal conversation among us, as He was before His passion among His disciples, with whom He commonly did eat and drink and talk.

Let us here deep consider the love of our Saviour Christ, which so loved His unto the end, that for their sakes He willingly suffered that painful end, and therein declared the highest point of love that can be. For as Himself saith: A greater love no man hath than to give his life for his friends. This is indeed the greatest love that ever any other man had. But yet had our Saviour a greater. For He gave His, and I said before, both for friend and foe.

But what a difference is there now between this faithful love of His and other kinds of false and fickle love used in this wretched world. The flatterer feigneth to love thee, for that he fareth well with thee. But now if adversity so minish thy substance that he find thy table unlaid, farewell, adieu, thy brother flatterer is gone, and getteth his to some other board, and yet shall turn sometime to thine enemy too and wait thee with a shrewd word.

Who can in adversity be sure of many of his friends when our Savior Himself was at His taking left alone and forsaken of His? When thou shalt go hence, who will go with thee? If thou were a king, will not all thy realm send thee forth alone and forget thee? Shall not thine own flesh let thee walk away, naked, silly soul, thou little wotest [knowest] whither?

Let us every man, therefore, in time learn to love, as we should, God above all thing and all other thing for Him. And whatsoever love be not referred to that end, that is to wit, to the pleasure of God it is a very vain and an unfruitful love. And whatsoever love we bear to any creature whereby we love God the less, that love is a loathsome love and hindereth us from heaven. Love no child of thine own so tenderly but that thou couldest be content so to sacrifice it to God as Abraham was ready with Isaac, if it so were that God would so command thee. And sith God will not so do, offer thy child otherwise to God's service. For whatsoever thing we love whereby we break God's commandment, that love we better than God – and that is a love deadly and damnable. Now, sith our Lord hath so loved us for our salvation, let us diligently call for His grace that against His great love we be not found unkind.

A prayer
O my sweet Saviour Christ, which, of Thine undeserved love toward mankind so kindly wouldest suffer the painful death of the cross, suffer not me to be cold nor lukewarm in love again toward Thee.

This consideration and prayer were written by Thomas More (1478–1535) during the fourteen months he remained imprisoned in the Tower before his execution. He feared sufferings and felt the miseries of imprisonment, but in his book The Dialogue of Comfort Against Tribulation, *and in his prayers and meditations, argued in favour of uniting himself with the sufferings of Christ rather than foolishly buying time in the world by betraying the law of God.*

The condemned man
John Gother

On the Day of Execution
When the last messenger of death comes, he ought to look upon him as bringing news of the spouse coming, and calling him to go forth and meet him. He ought in spirit to cry out *Paratum cor meum, Deus,* My heart is ready, O Lord, my heart is ready.

At the Place of Execution
I give myself wholly into thy hands, reject me not.
Now, Lord, according to thy good will, shew mercy to me.
Command my soul to be received in peace, for thou has redeemed
    me, O God of truth.

Lord Jesus, let these sweet words sound in my ears: 'This day thou
shalt be with me in paradise.'
O God, be merciful to me a sinner. O God, be merciful to me a
sinner.
Lord Jesus into thy hands I commend my spirit. Lord Jesus receive
my soul.

From Help for Prisoners, Especially for Those who are Condemned
to Die, *by John Gother, who died in 1704.*

Last affliction
William Dodd

Prayer before being hanged
Glory be to thee, oh God! for all the blessings thou hast granted
me from the day of my creation until the present hour;
I feel and adore thy exceeding goodness in all;
and in this last and closing affliction of my life, I acknowledge most
humbly the justice of thy fatherly correction, and bow my head
with thankfulness for thy rod!
Great and good in all! I adore and magnify thy mercy:
I behold in all thy love manifestly displayed;
and rejoice that I am at once thy creature and thy redeemed!
As such, oh Lord, my Creator and Redeemer, I commit my soul
into thy faithful hands!
Wash it and purify it in the blood of thy Son from every defiling
stain:
perfect what is wanting in it;
and grant me, poor, returning, weeping, wretched prodigal –
grant me the lowest place in thy heavenly house;
in and for his sole and all-sufficient merits – the adorable Jesus; –
who with the Father and the Holy Ghost liveth and reigneth
ever, one God, world without end!
Amen and Amen, Lord Jesus!

William Dodd (1729–77) was a clergyman condemned to death for forgery.
He had made a half-successful literary career, beginning with a poem on foot

and mouth disease called Diggon Davy's Resolution on the Death of his Last Cow *(1747). He got into debt and was convicted of forging a bill of exchange on which he had attempted to raise money. The jury recommended mercy, and many called for his reprieve, including Samuel Johnson, who had disliked his flashy way of life but opposed the fatal penalty. Johnson wrote speeches and prayers which were attributed to Dodd. He was hanged publicly at Tyburn on 27 June.*

Judgement
Liturgy of the Hours

Dies irae, dies illa,
solvet saeculum in favilla,
teste David cum Sibylla.

That day of wrath, that dreadful day,
shall heaven and earth in ashes lay,
as David and the Sybil say.

Quantus tremor est futurus,
quando iudex est venturus,
cuncta stricte discussurus!

What horror must invade the mind
when the approaching Judge shall find
and sift the deeds of all mankind!

Tuba mirum spargens sonum
per sepulcra regionum,
coget omnes ante thronum.

The mighty trumpet's wondrous tone
shall rend each tomb's sepulchral stone
and summon all before the Throne.

Mors stupebit et natura,
cum resurget creatura,
iudicanti responsura.

Now death and nature with surprise
behold the trembling sinners rise
to meet the Judge's searching eyes.

Liber scriptus proferetur,
in quo totum continetur,
unde mundus iudicetur.

Then shall with universal dread
the Book of Consciences be read
to judge the lives of all the dead.

*   *   *

Pie Iesu Domine,
dona eis requiem. Amen.

Lord, have mercy, Jesus blest,
grant them all Your Light and Rest. Amen.

The authorship of this chant, familiar both from church services and adaptation by composers, was once attributed to Thomas of Celano (1200–55), but is now generally ascribed to an unknown contemporary of his. The translation of the extract given here is partly based on those of James Ambrose Dominic Aylward (1813–72) and William F. Wingfield (1813–74). The verses derive in part from the biblical book of Zephaniah (1:14), 'The great day of the LORD *is near, it is near, and hasteth greatly, even the voice of the day of the* LORD: *the mighty man shall cry there bitterly. That day is a day of wrath, a day of trouble and distress, a day of wasteness and desolation, a day of darkness and gloominess, a day of clouds and thick darkness, a day of the trumpet and alarm against the fenced cities, and against the high towers.' Liturgically the* Dies Irae *is read or sung in the last week of the year, before Advent, which looks forward to the second coming of Jesus, as well as to his coming at Christmas.*

The Book of Life
Christina Rossetti

And I saw the dead, small and great, stand before God; and the
books were opened; and another book was opened, which is the
book of life: and the dead were judged out of those things which
were written in the books, according to their works. (Revelation
20:12)

On the dead for whom once Thou diedst, Lord Jesus, have mercy,
On the living for whom Thou ever livest, have mercy.
Thou Who wast arraigned before a corrupt judge, O Incorruptible
    Judge, have mercy.
Thou Who knowest what is in man, O Son of Man, have mercy.
Thou Whose works were all good, have mercy.
Thou Whose life, in the sight of the unwise, once hung in suspense
    before Pilate, have mercy.
Thou Who Thyself ever knowest what Thou wilt do, have mercy.
On the small, mercy.
On the great, mercy.
Thou Who art unlike us in Thy sinlessness, on us sinners
    have mercy.
Thou Who are like us in Thy Humanity, on us Thy brethren and
    Thy sisters, have mercy.
Blot out our evil works from Thy Book of Works, and have mercy.
Write our names in Thy Book of Life, and have mercy.
Blot not out our names, but have mercy.
Give us tears from the Fountain of Thy Mercy.
Store our tears in Thy bottle, with Thine own tears shed for us in
    pure mercy.
And whatever we lack let us not lack Thy mercy. Amen.

From The Face of the Deep *by Christina Rossetti (1830–94).*

Heaven and hell
Thomas Traherne

It was God's Wisdom made you Need the Sun.
It was His Goodness made you need the Sea.
Be Sensible of what you need, or Enjoy neither.
Consider how much you need them.
For thence they Derive their Value.
Suppose the Sun were Extinguished: or the Sea were Drie.
There would be no Light, no Beauty, no Warmth, no Fruits, no
    Flowers, no Pleasant Gardens, Feasts, or Prospects.
No Wine no Oyl no Bread, no Life, no Motion.
Would you not give all the Gold and Silver in the Indies for such a
    Treasure?
Prize it now you have it, at that Rate, and you shall be a Grateful
    Creature:
Nay you shall be a Divine and Heavenly Person.
For they in Heaven do Prize Blessings when they have them.
They in Earth when they have them Prize them not.
They in Hell Prize them, when they have them not.

To have Blessings and to Prize them is to be in Heaven;
To have them, and not to prize them, is to be in Hell, I would say
    upon Earth:
To prize them and not to have them, is to be in Hell.
Which is Evident by the Effects.
To Prize Blessings while we have them is to Enjoy them, and
    the effect thereof is Contentment, Pleasure, Thanksgiving,
    Happiness.
To Prize them when they are gone produceth Envy, Covetousness,
    Repining, Ingratitude, Vexation, Miserie.
But it was no Great Mistake to say, That to have Blessings, and not
    to Prize them is to be in Hell.
For it maketh them ineffectual, as if they were Absent.
Yea in some respect it is Worse then to be in Hell.
It is more vicious, and more Irrational.

These are numbers 46 and 47 in the First Century of Meditations *by
Thomas Traherne (1637–74)*

Lead me home
John Newton

Through many dangers, toils and snares
I have already come;
'Tis grace hath brought me safe thus far
And grace will lead me home.

John Newton (1725–1807) had been a slave trader and was moved to follow Christianity during an Atlantic storm. He became a Church of England clergyman and built up a large congregation at Olney, Buckinghamshire, to which the poet William Cowper moved to be near him. Though Cowper suffered from bouts of depression (for which Newton's Calvinism has unfairly been blamed), they compiled a volume entitled Olney Hymns, *which included Newton's 'Amazing Grace', which remains extremely popular.*

Resurrection of the body
St Patrick

And if at any time I managed anything of good for the sake of my
    God whom I love,
I beg of him that he grant it to me to shed my blood for his name
    with proselytes and captives,
even should I be left unburied,
or even were my wretched body to be torn limb from limb by dogs
    or savage beasts,
or were it to be devoured by the birds of the air,
I think, most surely, were this to have happened to me,
I had saved both my soul and my body.
For beyond any doubt on that day we shall rise again in the bright-
    ness of the sun,
that is, in the glory of Christ Jesus our Redeemer,
as children of the living God and co-heirs of Christ, made in his
    image;
for we shall reign through him and for him and in him.
For the sun we see rises each day for us at his command,

but it will never reign, neither will its splendour last,
but all who worship it will come wretchedly to punishment.
We, on the other hand, shall not die, who believe in and worship
   the true sun,
Christ, who will never die,
no more shall he die who has done Christ's will,
but will abide for ever just as Christ abides for ever,
who reigns with God the Father Almighty and with the Holy Spirit
before the beginning of time and now and for ever and ever.
Amen.

This extract from his Confession *is a genuine work of St Patrick, who lived in the fifth century and undertook the evangelization of Ireland, where his book was written.*

Sources and further reading

p. 2: Augustine of Hippo. I have updated E. B. Pusey's nineteenth-century translation of the *Confessions*, which itself was based firmly on that made by William Watts in 1631. Modern translations include F. J. Sheed (London: Continuum, Sheed and Ward, 1987). No one can do justice to Augustine's Latin, which is fluent, connected and nuanced.

　　The importance for subsequent centuries of theology of Augustine's reading of Psalm 4 is brought out by Fergus Kerr in his excellent *After Aquinas* (Oxford: Blackwell, 2002).

p. 8: Francis of Assisi. The translation here is adapted from traditional sources. For a good collection of Francis's works and early writings about him see *Saint Francis of Assisi: Omnibus of Sources*, 2 vols (Quincy, IL: Franciscan Press, Quincy University, 1991).

p. 9: Julian of Norwich. Adapted from *Revelations of Divine Love*, ed. Grace Warrack (London: Methuen, 1901), which is full of archaisms. There is also a translation by Elizabeth Spearing in Penguin Classics, which is a little easier to read and includes both the long and the short versions of the *Revelations* (taken from different manuscripts). An edition in Middle English is published by the Early English Text Sociey (Woodbridge: Boydell & Brewer).

p. 10: Christopher Smart. A scholarly edition of 'A Song to David' is given in *The Poetical Works of Christopher Smart, Volume II* (Oxford: Clarendon Press, 1983). A selection of Smart's poetry is available in Penguin Classics.

p. 12: Book of Common Prayer. The *First and Second Prayer Books of Edward VI* (1549 and 1552) are published by the Prayer Book Society (London, 1999). A full variety of versions of the Book of Common Prayer may be found at www.justus.anglican.org/resources/bcp.

p. 14: Frederick William Faber. From *The Creator and the Creature* (London: Burns and Oates, 1889). Burns and Oates reprinted the book in 1961, and it is fairly easy to find secondhand.

p. 15: Thomas Traherne. From *Centuries, Poems and Thanksgivings*, ed. H. M. Margoliouth (Oxford: Oxford University Press, 1958). Various selections can be found in paperback.

p. 18: Alcuin. This prayer appeared in a visitors' leaflet at York Minster. The standard Latin text of Alcuin's poetry is in *Poetae Latini Aevi Carolini*, ed. Ernst Dummler (Berlin, 1881). An excellent introduction to Alcuin's influence on the worship of the Church year is Gerald Ellard's *Master Alcuin, Liturgist* (Chicago: Loyola University Press, 1956).

p. 19: Augustine of Hippo. See note for page 2.

p. 20: Anselm. From *The Devotions of Saint Anselm*, ed. Clement C. J. Webb (London: Methuen, 1903). A paperback edition of the major works is available in Oxford World's Classics.

p. 20: Gerard Manley Hopkins. The poems and excerpts from the journals and letters are available in paperback as *The Major Works* (Oxford: Oxford University Press, 2002).

p. 21: John Henry Newman. From *Meditations and Devotions*. A neat edition is published as *Prayers, Verses and Devotions* (San Francisco: Ignatius Press, 1989).

p. 23: Lancelot Andrewes. I have used John Henry Newman's translation of the Greek prayers from *Bishop Andrewes' Preces Privatae* (Oxford: John Henry Parker, 1843); reprinted in *John Henry Newman, Prayers, Verses and Devotions* (San Francisco: Ignatius Press, 1989). Newman used the 1675 edition, and his translation appeared as Number 88 of the *Tracts for the Times*. A selection from this translation is available at www.justus.anglican.org/resources/pc/tracts/tract88.

The *Preces Privatae* were translated anew by F. E. Brightman (London: Methuen, 1903), who added the references for the origins of each phrase. A modern selection, translated by David Scott, is available in paperback (London: SPCK, 2002).

Andrewes' Ninety-Six Sermons was published by J. H. Parker (Oxford: Parker, 1841) and turns up secondhand. A small volume, *Selected Writings*, ed. P. E. Hewison, is published by Fyfield Books (Manchester, 1995).

p. 25: James Montgomery. From *Poems* (London: Routledge, Warne and Routledge, 1860). He figures in *Hymnwriters: Henry Baker, Albert Bayly, James Montgomery, John Newton* by Bernard Braley (London: Stainer and Bell, 1989).

p. 26: Book of Common Prayer (1549). See note for p. 12.

p. 26: Thomas Traherne. From *Centuries of Meditation*. See note for p. 15.

p. 27: John Chrysostom. The sermons in English translation are to be found secondhand in editions from the 1840s published by J. H. Parker (Oxford).

p. 28: Thomas Ken. From *The Practice of Divine Love: An Exposition upon the Church Catechism* (London and Oxford: A. R. Mowbray, 1907). *Prose Works of Thomas Ken*, ed. Revd W. Benham (London: Griffith, Farren, Okenden & Welsh, 1889) includes his *Manual of Prayers for Winchester Scholars*, and the latter is available at www.justus.anglican.org. I am unable to find Ken's writings in print.

p. 34: Book of Common Prayer (1662). Many editions exist, both new and secondhand. Everyman's Library Classics appends the 1549 Communion service and contains a useful introduction.

p. 34: Walter Hilton. Modernized from *The Scale (or Ladder) of Perfection*

(London, 1870). This is a version of Serenus Cressy's seventeenth-century translation of the classic. His book had been printed in English in the last decade of the fifteenth century by Wynkyn de Worde, Caxton's collaborator. Today it is available in several editions, newly translated, though it is hard to preserve both the freshness of Hilton's prose and the technical vocabulary that clothes his thought.

p. 35: Book of Common Prayer (1662). See note for p. 34.

p. 36: John Keble. From *A Daily Text-Book, Gathered from the Sermons for the Christian Year* by the Revd John Keble, by E. H. and F. H. (London: Walter Smith, 1884). A selection of the sermons has been made by Maria Poggi Johnson, and is available in paperback: *Sermons of the Christian Year* (Grand Rapids, MI: Eerdmans 2004).

p. 36: Christopher Smart. This famous passage appears in paperback selections from Smart. A scholarly edition of the 'Jubilate Agno' makes up Volume I of *The Poetical Works* (Oxford: Clarendon Press, 1980).

p. 39: George MacDonald. From *A Book of Strife in the Form of The Diary of an Old Soul*. This is in print from various publishers in hardback and paperback, and available cheaply as a download. But a free version, with a few misprints, may also be found on the internet.

p. 40: William Caxton. *The Golden Legend* was Caxton's own heavily edited version (1483) of the immensely popular devotional work by Jacobus de Voragine (1275). There is a pretty edition in seven little volumes in the Temple Classics series (London: J. M. Dent, 1900). Even prettier is William Morris's three-volume Kelmscott edition of 1892, which sells at auction for £1,000 or so. But Caxton's text can be read free on the internet at www.fordham.edu/halsall/basis/goldenlegend.

p. 42: Girolamo Savonarola. From *The Lord's Prayer and the Angelical Salutation by Father Jerome Savonarola* (London: Catholic Truth Society, 1899). There was a fashion for Savonarola in the nineteenth century, when several collections of his writings were published in English; I cannot find that any are in print now, even though he has recently gone through a rehabilitation.

p. 43: Thomas Traherne. From *Centuries of Meditation*. See note for p. 15.

p. 45: John Kettlewell. From *The Churchman's Companion in the Closet* (New York: Stanford and Delisser, 1858), ed. Francis Paget, the clergyman author of remarkable novels such as *St Antholin's* (1841) and *Milford Malvoisin, or, Pews and Pewholders* (1842).

p. 48: J. M. Neale. An edition of *Hymns Ancient and Modern* is published by Canterbury Press (Norwich).

p. 49: John Henry Newman. See note for p. 21.

p. 51: Giles Fletcher. *The Poetical Works of Giles and Phineas Fletcher* was published by Cambridge University Press in 1909, and reprinted in 1970.

p. 52: John Byrom. His poems were collected in editions in 1773 and 1814, but I do not think they are in print now. Some appear in anthologies and others in hymn books.

p. 52: Robert Southwell. The standard text of his poetry is *The Poems of Robert Southwell*, SJ, ed. James H. McDonald (Oxford: Clarendon Press, 1967). It has gone out of print (as have other editions).

p. 53: The Missal. The 1962 Roman Missal is published with English translation by Angelus Press, Kansas City, MO.

p. 54: Columba Marmion. From *Christ in His Mysteries* (London: Sands & Co, 1939).

p. 55: Liturgy of the Hours. The text before the reforms of the Second Vatican Council was published in many editions, such as *The Hours of the Divine Office in English and Latin* (Collegeville, MN: Liturgical Press, 1963). The current *Liturgia Horarum* is published by the Libreria Editrice Vaticana (Vatican City, 1985).

p. 55: Christina Rossetti. From *Time Flies: A Reading Diary* (London: Society for Promoting Christian Knowledge, 1885). Her poems are in print from several paperback publishers. Four volumes of her religious prose works (*Called to be Saints: The Minor Festivals Devotionally Studied; Letter and Spirit: Notes on the Commandments; Time Flies: A Reading Diary; and The Face of the Deep: A Devotional Commentary on The Apocalypse*) have been edited by Maria Keaton (Chicago: Thoemmes Continuum, 2003). *Selected Prose of Christina Rossetti* was edited by David A. Kent and P. G Stanwood (London: Macmillan, 1998).

p. 56: Book of Common Prayer. See note for p. 34.

p. 57: Frederick William Faber. From *The Creator and the Creature*. See note for p. 14.

p. 58: Book of Common Prayer. See note for p. 34.

p. 58: Ronald Knox. Most of his devotional books are easy to find secondhand. *The Hidden Stream: The Mysteries of the Christian Faith* is published by Ignatius Press (San Francisco, 2002).

p. 59: Alcuin. The Latin and a different translation of this and other verses is to be found in *More Latin Lyrics* by Helen Waddell (London: Victor Gollancz, 1976). See also her *Mediaeval Latin Lyrics* (London: Constable, 1929; later published in paperback by Penguin). Douglas Dales has translated some of Alcuin's prayers and writing about prayer in *A Mind Intent on God: the Spiritual Writings of Alcuin of York* (Norwich: Canterbury Press, 2004).

p. 60: Orthodox Liturgy of the Hours. A useful website for Orthodox services in English is www.sspeterpaul.org/priest. More prayers can be found at www.myriobiblos.gr/texts/english/prayerbook/main.

p. 60: Thomas Traherne. See note for p. 15.

p. 62:   Venantius Fortunatus. Some of his verse is to be found in *The Oxford Book of Medieval Latin Verse*, ed. F. J. E. Raby (Oxford: Clarendon Press, 1959). See also *Venantius Fortunatus: Personal and Political Poems*, translated and introduced by Judith George (Oxford: Oxbow Books, 2005).

p. 64:   John Henry Newman. *The Dream of Gerontius* is available in paperback from St Pauls Publishing (London, 2001).

p. 65:   Henry Baker. For *Hymns Ancient and Modern* see note for p. 48. Baker figures in *Hymnwriters: Henry Baker, Albert Bayly, James Montgomery, John Newton* by Bernard Braley (London: Stainer and Bell, 1989).

p. 66.   Anselm. See note for p. 20.

p. 67.   Jacopone da Todi. Songs attributed to Jacopone and his contemporaries are published in a translation by Serge and Elizabeth Hughes under the title *The Lauds*, in the Classics of Western Spirituality series (Paulist Press: Mahwah, NJ, 1981).

p. 68.   Book of Common Prayer. See note for p. 12

p. 68.   Isaac Watts. *The Psalms and Hymns of Isaac Watts* is published by Soli Deo Gloria Ministries (Orlando, FL, 2003), but can be found more cheaply in nineteenth-century editions.

p. 69:   Anima Christi. The Latin version and other Latin prayers are available at www.home.earthlink.net/~thesaurus/index.

p 71:   The sign of the Cross. An interesting chapter on this Christian custom may be found in *Familiar Prayers* by Herbert Thurston (London: Burns and Oates, 1953).

p. 71:   Before a crucifix. The Latin version may be found on the same internet site as the Anima Christi (see note for p. 69).

p. 71:   The Missal. See note for p. 53.

p. 72:   Book of Common Prayer. See note for p. 34.

p. 72:   Joseph Beaumont. *The Complete Poems*, ed. Alexander Grosart, was published in 1880, and was produced in facsimile by AMS Press (New York, 1967). The 'Easter Dialogue' was published in a curious book of verse edited by Edmund Blunden and Bernard Mellor, dominated by selections from *Tixall Poetry* (see note on 'Dwelling in Hearts', below, and published as *Wayside Poems of the Seventeenth Century* (Hong Kong: Hong Kong University Press, 1963), which is easy to find secondhand. Beaumont wrote a 30,000-line epic called 'Psyche, or The Soul's Mystery', which takes up the bulk of his *Complete Poems*, in which is printed not the first edition of 1648 but the version he revised before his death (sometimes the revision is blamed on his son, but that seems not to be true).

p. 75:   The Missal. See note for p. 53.

p. 76:   George Herbert. *The Complete English Works* are available in economical hardback from Everyman's Library (London: 1995).

p. 77:   Liturgy of the Hours. See note for p. 55.

p. 77:   The Missal. See note for p. 53.

p. 78:   Lady Lucy Herbert. From *The Devotions of the Lady Lucy Herbert of Powis*, ed. John Morris SJ (London: Burns and Oates, 1873).

p. 78:   John Keble. See note for p. 36.

p. 79:   Thomas Aquinas. The text here is as used in the Roman Missal. A variant text may be found in *The Oxford Book of Medieval Latin Verse*, ed. F. J. E. Raby (Oxford: Clarendon Press, 1959).

p. 81:   Richard Challoner. Another perennially popular manual by Challoner was *Think Well On't, or, Reflections on the Great Truths of the Christian Religion, for Every Day of the Year*. The historian Eamon Duffy edited a collection of essays: *Challoner and his Church* (London: Darton, Longman and Todd, 1981).

p. 82:   Christina Rossetti. See note for p. 55.

p. 83:   Catherine Winkworth. *Lyra Germanica* can still easily be found in nineteenth-century editions.

p. 84:   Anon. Edmund Bishop's translation and essay are in *Liturgica Historica* (Oxford: Clarendon Press, 1917). The prayer book had been split into two manuscript books, both now belonging to the British Library, called Cotton Galba A.xiv and Cotton Nero A.ii. The manuscripts, collected by Sir Robert Cotton (1571–1631), take their name from the Roman Emperors' busts that stood on his bookcases. In 1731 a fire broke out at Ashburnham House where they were kept, which charred some leaves (along with the sole manuscript of *Beowulf*). In 1865 another fire, at a binder's, utterly destroyed other Galba manuscripts. The two manuscripts are printed as Volume 103 of the Henry Bradshaw Society's series, as *A Pre-Conquest English Prayer-Book*, ed. Bernard James Muir (1988).

p. 85:   Book of Common Prayer. See note for p. 34.

p. 86:   Thomas Traherne. See note for p. 15.

p. 87:   Book of Common Prayer. See note for p. 34.

p. 88:   Robert Herrick. From *The Poetical Works*, ed. F. W. Moorman (Oxford: Oxford University Press, 1915). Selections are in print in various paperback editions.

p. 88:   George MacDonald. See note for p. 39.

p. 89:   Book of Common Prayer. See note for p. 34

p. 89:   Richard Challoner. See note for p. 81.

p. 93:   Book of Common Prayer. See note for p. 34.

p. 93:   Christina Rossetti. See note for p. 55.

p. 94:   Book of Common Prayer. See note for p. 34.

p. 94: John Keble. See note for p. 36.

p. 94: Book of Common Prayer. See note for p. 34.

p. 95: J. G. Whittier. *Selected Poems by John Greenleaf Whittier* is published by Library of America (New York, NY, 2004). The complete poems are very common secondhand.

p. 96: Book of Common Prayer. See note for p. 34

p. 96: Anselm. See note for p. 20.

p. 97: Henry Vaughan. From *The Works of Henry Vaughan*, ed. Leonard Cyril Martin (Oxford: Oxford University Press, 1914). *Selected Poems* is published by SPCK (London, 2004).

p. 98: Book of Common Prayer. See note for p. 34.

p. 99: Anselm. See note for p. 20.

p. 100: John Austin. Old editions of *Devotions in the Ancient Way of Offices* may be found. Beyond the *Dictionary of National Biography*, not much about John Austin has been published. There is, however, a doctoral thesis by P. H. Pfatteicher, 'The life and writings of John Austin' (University of Pennsylvania, 1966).

p. 101: William Caxton. See note for p. 40.

p. 103: George Hickes. Some of Hickes's philological works were republished in facsimile in the 1970s, but not his devotional works.

p. 104: Gerard Manley Hopkins. See note for p. 20.

p. 105: John Donne. A well-printed edition of the *Devotions upon Emergent Occasions*, ed. John Sparrow, was published by Cambridge University Press in 1923. A paperback, edited by Andrew Motion, is published by Vintage Books (London, 1999).

p. 109: John Keble. See note for p. 36.

p. 110: Christina Rossetti. See note for p. 55.

p. 111: Henry Vaughan. See note for p. 97.

p. 112: Book of Common Prayer. See note for p. 34. For the *Magnificat* see the *Biblia Sacra Iuxta Vulgatam Versionem* (Stuttgart: Deutsche Bibelgesellschaft, 1990), which I mention because it can be bought on the internet via Amazon. The Bible in Latin is not commonly found in bookshops, but can often be ordered.

p. 113: Aldhelm. The standard edition of Aldhelm, in the Monumenta Germaniae Historica series, was edited by R. Ehwald (Berlin, 1919). *Aldhelm, the Poetic Works*, translated by Michael Lapidge and James L. Rosier (Woodbridge: D. S. Brewer, 1985) is also out of print.

p. 114: Book of Common Prayer. See note for p. 34.

p. 114: Hilaire Belloc. From *Sonnets and Verse* (London: Duckworth, 1945).

p. 115: Alcuin. See note for p. 59.

p. 116: Hermann Contractus. For more on the 'Salve' see Herbert Thurston, *Familiar Prayers* (London: Burns and Oates, 1953).

p. 116: John Paul II. From *The Seafarers' Prayer Book*, published by the Apostleship of the Sea, Herald House, Lamb's Passage, Bunhill Row, London EC1Y 8LE. Among selections from Pope John Paul's writings is *Breakfast with the Pope: 120 Daily Readings* (New York: Gramercy Books, 2003). For full texts of his letters, beginning with *Redemptor Hominis*, see the Holy See website www.vatican.va/phome_en.

p. 117: Traditional. For more on the 'Memorare' see Herbert Thurston, *Familiar Prayers* (London: Burns and Oates, 1953).

p. 118: Book of Common Prayer. See note for p. 34.

p. 118: Augustine Baker. From *Holy Wisdom, Extracted out of more than Forty Treatises and Methodically Digested by Serenus Cressy* (1657), ed. Abbot Sweeney (London: Burns and Oates, 1911). This was republished in the Orchard Series (Burns and Oates), and again by A. Clarke Books in 1972.

p. 120: John Henry Newman. See note for p. 21.

p. 120: Christopher Smart. A scholarly edition of *Hymns and Spiritual Songs for the Fasts and Festivals of the Church of England* is given in *The Poetical Works of Christopher Smart*, Volume II (Oxford: Clarendon Press, 1983).

p. 123: Leo XIII. The Latin may be found in the Roman Missal of 1962. See note for p. 53.

p. 126: God be in my head. Anonymous. For the use of the primer in popular devotion see *The Stripping of the Altars* by Eamon Duffy (London: Yale University Press, 1992). For subsequent developments see J. M. Blom, *The post-Tridentine English primer* (London: Catholic Record Society, 1982).

p. 126: Dwelling in hearts. Anonymous. From *Tixall Poetry*, ed. Arthur Clifford (Edinburgh: John Ballantyne, 1813).

p. 127: Augustine of Hippo. For the *Confessions* see note for p. 2.

p. 128: R. H. Benson. From *Poems* (London: Burns and Oates, 1914).

p. 129: Ronald Knox. See note for p. 58.

p. 130: John Bunyan. George Offor's big three-volume edition of *Bunyan's Works* (London, 1862) is still useful. Oxford University Press has been issuing expensive volumes of a learned edition: *The Poems*, ed. Graham Midgeley, was published as one volume (Oxford: Oxford University Press, 1980). The *Pilgrim's Progress* is in print in paperback.

p. 132: Thomas Traherne. See note for p. 15.

p. 132: John Henry Newman. The meditations of which this formed a part were published in 1893, after Newman's death. They may be found in *Prayers, Verses and Devotions* (San Francisco: Ignatius Press, 1989), or secondhand.

p. 138: Traditional. The Apostles' Creed. For medieval use of the creed, see *The*

Stripping of the Altars by Eamon Duffy (London: Yale University Press, 1992).

p. 139: John Gother. From *The Spiritual Works of the Rev John Gother* (Newcastle, 1792).

p. 140: Book of Common Prayer. See note for p. 34.

p. 141: Lady Lucy Herbert. See note for p. 78.

p. 141: The Missal. See note for p. 53.

p. 142: Book of Common Prayer. See note for p. 34.

p. 142: Thomas Traherne. See note for p. 15.

p. 144: Robert Herrick. See note for p. 88.

p. 144: Jane Austen. This is one of three evening prayers known to have been written by Jane Austen. These are reprinted in *Volume VI: Minor Works* of R. W. Chapman's edition of *The Works of Jane Austen* (Oxford: Oxford University Press, 1954). Another source is *Jane Austen: Catharine and Other Writings*, ed. Margaret Anne Doody and Douglas Murray (Oxford: Oxford World's Classics, 1993), an excellent paperback edition of Jane Austen's shorter works.

p. 145: Jeremy Taylor. From *The Whole Works of the Right Rev Jeremy Taylor DD*, Volume VIII (London, 1883).

p. 146: William Cowper. From *The Poetical Works of William Cowper* (London: Henry Frowde, Oxford University Press, 1911). Selected poems are available in paperback. A selection of Cowper's letters tracing his life is published by Carcanet (www.carcanet.co.uk).

p. 147: Christina Rossetti. See note for p. 55.

p. 148: Mother Teresa. A selection of her prayers and teaching may be found in the inexpensive paperback *A Fruitful Branch on the Vine, Jesus* (Cincinnati, OH: St Anthony Messenger Press, 2000).

p. 149: Jane Austen. See note for p. 144.

p. 149: Book of Common Prayer. See note for p. 34.

p. 150: John Henry Newman. From *Verses on Various Occasions*, under the title 'The Pillar of Cloud'. In *Prayers, Verses and Devotions* (San Francisco: Ignatius Press, 1989) or secondhand.

p. 151: Book of Common Prayer. See note for p. 34.

p. 151: Anonymous. For St Patrick, see *The Life and Writings of the Historical Saint Patrick*, ed. and translated by R. P. C. Hanson (New York: Seabury Press, 1983).

p. 154: Christina Rossetti. See note for p. 55.

p. 154: *The Seafarers' Prayer Book*. Published by the Apostleship of the Sea, Herald House, Lamb's Passage, Bunhill Row, London EC1Y 8LE.

p. 156: Robert Herrick. See note for p. 88.

p. 156: Traditional. Grace before meals. For more, see Reginald Adams, *The College Graces of Oxford and Cambridge* (Oxford: Perpetua Press, 1992).

p. 157: William Walsham How. For his life see F. D. How, *Bishop Walsham How: a Memoir* (London: Isbister & Co, 1899).

p. 159: *The Seafarers' Prayer Book*. See note for p. 154.

p. 160: Susanna Wesley. The hymn 'What! Never speak on evil word' appears in full in the 1876 editon of *A Collection of Hymns for the use of the People called Methodists* (London: Wesleyan-Methodist Book Room, 1889). Michael McMullen has edited a modern collection of *Prayers and Meditations of Susanna Wesley* (London: Methodist Publishing House, 2000).

p. 161: Robert Louis Stevenson. From *Prayers Written at Vailima* (London: Chatto & Windus, 1904).

p. 162: Lancelot Andrewes. John Henry Newman's translation of the Greek prayers from *Bishop Andrewes' Preces Privatae* (Oxford: John Henry Parker, 1843). It is reprinted in *John Henry Newman, Prayers, Verses and Devotions* (San Francisco: Ignatius Press, 1989).

p. 167: Henry Vaughan. See note for p. 97.

p. 168: Liturgy of the Hours. See note for p. 55.

p. 169: Alcuin. The Latin and a different translation of this and other verses is to be found in *More Latin Lyrics* by Helen Waddell (London: Victor Gollancz, 1976).

p. 169: Book of Common Prayer. See note for p. 34.

p. 169: John Wesley. From *The Works of the Rev John Wesley* (London: Wesleyan Methodist Bookroom, 1872). There is a good introductory biography: *John Wesley, a Personal Portrait* by Ralph Waller (London: SPCK, 2003).

p. 171: Jane Austen. See note for p. 144.

p. 172: *The Seafarers' Prayer Book*. See note for p. 154.

p. 173: Hannah More. From *The Works of Hannah More*, Volume II (London: T. Cadell, 1830).

p. 173: William Cowper. See note for p. 146.

p. 174: Lancelot Andrewes. See note for p. 162.

p. 180: Book of Common Prayer. See note for p. 34.

p. 181: Augustine of Hippo. From the *Confessions*. See note for p. 2.

p. 181: John Donne. His poetry is in print in a variety of editions.

p. 182: Samuel Johnson. The standard edition is *Diaries, Prayers and Annals*, ed. E. L. McAdam (New Haven, CT: Yale University Press, 1958).

p. 183: Book of Common Prayer. See note for p. 34.

p. 183: Thomas More. A good edition of the 'Treatise upon the Passion' is in *The Tower Works: Devotional Writings*, ed. Garry E. Haupt (London: Yale University Press, 1980).

p. 185: John Gother. From *The Spiritual Works of the Rev John Gother* (Newcastle, 1792).

p. 186: William Dodd. From *Thoughts in Prison* (London: Printed for C. Cooke, 1796).

p. 187: Liturgy of the Hours. The full Latin text of the 'Dies Irae' is present in Missals from before 1962, and in the current *Liturgia Horarum*.

p. 189: Christina Rossetti. See note for p. 55.

p. 190: Thomas Traherne. See note for p. 15.

p. 191: John Newton figures in *Hymnwriters: Henry Baker, Albert Bayly, James Montgomery, John Newton* by Bernard Braley (London: Stainer and Bell, 1989).

p. 191: St Patrick. See *The Life and Writings of the Historical Saint Patrick*, ed. and translated by R. P. C. Hanson (New York: Seabury Press, 1983).